A SEPARATE PENSION PLAN FOR ALBERTA

Analysis and Discussion

INSTITUTE FOR PUBLIC ECONOMICS

A Separate Pension Plan for Alberta

Analysis and Discussion

The University
of Alberta Press

Western Studies in Economic Policy No. 5

EDITED BY PAUL BOOTHE

OBN 1627888

Published by
The University of Alberta Press
Ring House 2
Edmonton, Alberta
T6G 2E1

Copyright © 2000 The University of Alberta Press
Printed in Canada 5 4 3 2 1
ISBN 0-88864-351-9

CANADIAN CATALOGUING IN PUBLICATION DATA

Main entry under title:
   A separate pension plan for Alberta
   (Western studies in economic policy ; no. 5)
   Includes bibliographical references.
   ISBN 0-88864-351-9

   1. Pensions—Canada. 2. Pensions—Alberta. 3. Canada Pension Plan. I. Boothe, Paul Michael,
1954- II. Series.
HD7105.35.C3S46 2000   368.4'3'00971   C00-910285-X

Printed and bound in Canada by Hignell Book Printing, Winnipeg, Manitoba.
∞ Printed on acid-free paper.

The University of Alberta Press gratefully acknowledges the support received for its program
from the Canada Council for the Arts. The Press also acknowledges the financial support of the
Government of Canada through the Book Publishing Industry Development Program for its
publishing activities.

Canadä

HD
7105.35
.C2
S46
2000

Contents

PAUL BOOTHE

Introduction

IN THE FIRST HALF of the 1990s Canadians became aware that the Canada Pension Plan (CPP), our mandatory public pension scheme, was in serious trouble. The root causes of the trouble were that benefits were paid out long before the early recipients had contributed enough to cover the cost of such benefits and that the scope of benefits was expanded substantially over time—for example to cover persons with disabilities—without a corresponding increase in contributions. Political leaders realized that without a substantial increase in contribution rates, the CPP would run out of money.

This realization brought about a long series of negotiations between federal and provincial governments that culminated in the reforms agreed upon in 1997 and implemented on January 1, 1999. These reforms included increasing contribution rates from 5.6 percent in 1996 to 9.9 percent in 2003 and having an independent investment board invest contributions in market instruments rather than the continuing the current practice of buying provincial government bonds bearing the federal borrowing rate.

Alberta was one of eight provinces that agreed to the changes (Saskatchewan and British Columbia did not). Indeed, Alberta played an important role in brokering the deal; however a substantial body of opinion remained within and outside the province that the reforms did not go far enough. A number of commentators have argued that reforms should have moved the CPP further in the direction of a mandatory fully funded private pension plan, and the intergenerational transfer from younger to older workers and retirees inherent in the current scheme be redressed. Others have countered that recent reforms will be sufficient and should be allowed to work.

This volume considers the question regarding public pensions from an Alberta perspective. Specifically, it deals with four questions:

1. What are the remaining problems with the recently reformed CPP?
2. What has been Québec's experience with Canada's only provincially administered public pension plan?
3. What are the costs and benefits of a provincial public pension plan administered by the Province of Alberta?

4. From the perspective of the rest of Canada, is a move to an Alberta pension plan administratively feasible and desirable?

To answer these questions, the Institute for Public Economics assembled experts from across Canada. Bill Robson of the C.D. Howe Institute looked the recent CPP reforms and remaining problems with Canada's public pension system. Québec's pension plan was examined by François Vaillancourt of Université de Montreal. The pros and cons of an Alberta pension plan were considered by Herb Emery and Ken McKenzie of the University of Calgary. Finally, Robert Brown from the University of Waterloo looked at the feasibility and desirability of an Alberta pension plan from a Canadian perspective.

Initial versions of the studies in this volume were presented in an Institute-sponsored conference in January of 1999. Participants included academics, public servants, and business people. A second group of eminent people were enlisted to lead the discussion of the papers. That group included Michael Prince from University of Victoria, and Ken Norrie, Mel McMillan, and Randall Morck from University of Alberta. Bev Dahlby of the University of Alberta provided a synthesis of the day's discussion (which is reproduced as the final chapter of this volume). Special thanks are also due to Alberta Treasury for financial support that made this research project possible.

■■■■ OVERVIEW OF THE STUDIES

Bill Robson's study, "Precarious Pyramid: The Economics and Politics of the CPP," lays out the remaining problems with the recently reformed CPP. Robson begins with a look at the initial structure of the CPP and why it was unsustainable, and then discusses the reforms that were enacted in 1997.

In Robson's view, the 1997 reforms do not go far enough. Compared to the returns possible in a private pension plan, the reformed CPP still represents a 40 percent tax on young workers even if they believe that all promised future CPP payments will actually be made. Further, Robson expresses concern over possible political constraints on the CPP Investment Board, on the sustainability of the 9.9 percent contribution rate, and on the outcome of the current federal-provincial review of CPP. Robson believes that more radical reforms may yet be needed. He argues that Canadians should consider, for example, shifting to a broader tax base (such as personal income tax) to fund existing obligations and moving to individual, fully funded retirement accounts for the young. Finally, Robson sees a key role for Alberta in the ongoing reform process. With the youngest population and a high employment rate, Alberta is the province that can make the most credible threat to withdraw from the current CPP if the reform process does not continue. This threat, he argues, may provide Ottawa and some provinces with the incentive to continue the reform process to forestall Alberta's departure from the CPP.

François Vaillancourt' study, "The Québec Pension Plan: Institutional Arrangements and Lessons for Alberta," begins by laying out the historical evolution and operations of the QPP. Drawing from the experience in Québec in three different areas, Vaillancourt proposes six lessons for Alberta:

1. A provincial pension plan gives greater flexibility to the province with respect to the retirement aspects of social policy. This flexibility allowed the Province of Québec to more easily abolish mandatory retirement as it could vary the age of access to QPP.
2. A provincial pension plan changes the incentive for provincial governments to shift the burden of disability benefits to federally funded programs. Vaillancourt argues that the incentive for provinces to shift the burden of disability benefits from provincial welfare programs to pensions is mitigated when both programs are administered by the provincial government.
3. The large investment pool that accompanies a provincial pension plan can be used to increase local control of the economy. Thus in Québec the government used the QPP effectively to increase francophone ownership and participation in the Québec economy.
4. The large investment pool that accompanies a provincial pension plan can be used to develop a local financial services industry. Vaillancourt argues believes the need to invest the contributions to the QPP encouraged the development of the Québec financial sector.
5. The large investment pool that accompanies a provincial pension plan permits the provincial government to intervene in financial markets in times of heightened uncertainty. Using the investment pool, government can intervene to mitigate negative reaction to government policies by financial markets.
6. A provincial pension plan should be free from day-to-day managerial interference, but should be subject to overall public policy directives. It is important that provincial pension fund managers be free to react to financial market conditions as they develop. However, provincial goals should be paramount in determining the overall direction of investment policy.

In "Checking Out of the Hotel California: The Desirability of an Alberta Pension Plan," Herb Emery and Ken McKenzie analyze two alternative Alberta Pension Plans (APPs). The first alternative is one where the APP has the same essential structure as the existing CPP, but takes advantage of

Alberta's favourable demographics and high employment rate. The second alternative is a radical departure from the current CPP: a fully funded pension plan for Alberta.

Focusing on the first alternative, Emery and McKenzie argue that the demographic advantage enjoyed by Alberta is not as large as commonly assumed. The median age of the Alberta population is 33 compared to 35 for all of Canada. Emery and McKenzie estimate that this age advantage could permit a reduction of premiums of about 1.75 percent from the target of 9.9 percent under CPP. Balanced against this age advantage would be the higher administrative costs and loss of diversification that would accompany a separate APP. Furthermore, Emery and McKenzie argue that Alberta's disadvantage in the current CPP is intergenerational rather than interregional. It is because of youth, not place of residence, that the average Albertan will be required to contribute disproportionately to the benefits they receive. Older Albertans will benefit in the same way as older workers and pensioners from other parts of Canada.

Emery and McKenzie next examine a radical departure from the current CPP: a fully funded APP. They argue that full funding makes the transition from the current system even more difficult. Given the need to guarantee the unfunded benefits of older workers, they estimate that only workers currently under 30 years of age would actually benefit from full funding. Emery and McKenzie conclude that while further pension reform may be desirable, it is best pursued at the federal rather than at the provincial level.

Robert Brown begins his chapter by looking at the feasibility of Alberta opting out of the CPP. Legally, any province is free to set up its own pension plan provided that the plan is "similar" to the CPP. However, the federal legislation is not specific regarding what "similar" actually means. Any changes that would have a material impact on the CPP (including opting out) would require the approval of at least two-thirds of the provinces representing two-thirds of the Canadian population.

Financially, any province opting out would be required to assume its share of the net liability. Brown estimates Alberta's share to be approximately $46 billion dollars. Finally, Brown argues that the current political environment (especially with the current governments of Ontario and Québec) and the relatively uncomplicated nature of CPP assets (provincial government bonds) might make it easier for Alberta to opt out now than in the future.

Despite the feasibility of opting out, Brown argues strongly that it would not be in Alberta's or Canada's interest for Alberta to do so. He points to the success of the current system in reducing poverty among the elderly and to its broad coverage, immediate vesting, portability, and low administrative costs. Further, he shows that a fully funded pension scheme would not be immune to the demographic shifts underlying concerns regarding the current system. Finally, he argues that a fully funded provincial scheme would most likely forego the ancillary benefits of the current system (such as disability benefits and the pooling of risk) and face higher administration costs. Therefore, Brown thinks that Alberta's best course of action is to work within the current system to ensure a viable national public pension scheme.

The final chapter in the volume is written by Bev Dahlby of the Institute for Public Economics. Dahlby accepted the unenviable but essential role of drawing the lessons from each of the studies, highlighting areas where he agreed or disagreed. He suggests that independent retirement accounts (IRAs) may provide an alternative to the CPP, as indicated in the World Bank model. This model consists of 3 pillars: a mandatory public pension (such as Canada's Old Age Security), mandatory contributions to independent retirement accounts (instead of contributions to the CPP), and voluntary savings (such as RRSPs). Dahlby also identifies issues that still need to be considered before Alberta makes a decision on whether or not to set up a separate provincial pension plan.

WILLIAM B.P. ROBSON

Precarious Pyramid

The Economics and Politics of the CPP

THE CANADA PENSION PLAN (CPP) is a largely unfunded, earnings-related pension plan. Aside from a buffer of funds intended to equal two years of payouts, current benefits are financed, not by assets purchased in advance, but by the contributions of current workers. It was established in the mid-1960s, a period when income growth exceeded the yields on debt securities—circumstances that appeared to support a Ponzi-style scheme. The re-emergence of a more normal environment of interest rates that exceed economic growth rates put the CPP under stress. Without steady increases in contribution rates, money to pay benefits would run out. With them, however, younger workers in particular were being promised a benefit package at retirement that fell far short of what they could have earned by making the same contributions to a funded plan. A large portion—perhaps most—of CPP premiums paid by such workers was effectively a tax.

To the extent that CPP premiums feel like taxes, they drive a wedge between what employers pay and what employees take home, hurting work incentives, cutting into business cashflows, and encouraging work in the underground economy. They are also unpopular, creating political pressure for reforms to lighten or eliminate them. Thus, a vicious circle threatens: the more participants doubt they will see their benefits, the more tax-like premiums become.

Starting in 1992, a combination of flagging growth in contributions and a disability-driven explosion of expenditures began to deplete the plan's buffer. Combined with a growing sense that the plan might be unsustainable, this depletion spurred action on reforms. The resulting package, implemented in 1998, aimed to fund the CPP more fully by expanding the contribution base, hiking rates, and trimming benefits. It also set up an arm's-length board to administer the larger fund of assets.

The reform package lessened the CPP's tilt against the young, but the key question is whether it will improve confidence that the plan will pay its obligations in full. If it does, the rise in premiums now under way will be less damaging, since the premiums will feel less like taxes and therefore will reduce their economic cost and stem the erosion of political support for the plan. If it does not, the damage from the high premiums will be greater, and support for the plan will continue to erode.

Among the factors likely to influence confidence in the CPP over the next few years are the activities of the CPP Investment Board, the outcome of the current federal-provincial review of the CPP's structure, and the durability of the 9.9 percent contribution rate. My necessarily speculative judgement is that the net impact of the first will be neutral, the second may be negative, and the third is likely to be negative, since there are reasons for doubting that the optimistic assessment of the recent 17th Actuarial Report will be borne out.

If that is right, it makes sense to prepare for more radical reforms that might inspire more confidence among Canadians. Such reforms might look to mandatory but individually controlled retirement accounts to finance benefits that will accrue in the future and might shift to broader tax bases to finance obligations that already exist. Individual provinces can play a key role in this process: the possibility that a province might opt out of the existing plan might appear an attractive guarantee to its citizens, and a credible threat to do so might encourage better behaviour on the part of the other governments jointly responsible for the CPP. No province is better placed to play such a role than Alberta.

BUILDING A PYRAMID

The CPP is a compulsory, government-run, earnings-related pension plan. It collects contributions on all employment earnings between the Year's Maximum Pensionable Earnings (YMPE—roughly equal to the average wage) and the Year's Basic Exemption (YBE—a low-income threshold equal to roughly one-tenth the YMPE). Payment of contributions is split, with employers and employees each responsible for one half. The CPP pays a variety of retirement, survivor, orphan, and disability benefits calculated either with reference to the YMPE or flat-rate schedules. It began both collecting contributions and paying out (partial) benefits in 1966.

The Ponzi-Style Design
Although the CPP began paying full retirement benefits only in 1976, the fact that payouts began at the plan's inception was central to its design. Following its running-in period, the plan was intended to maintain only a small buffer of funds, equal to roughly two years of payouts, to deal with unexpected swings in contributions or benefits. Unlike registered retirement saving plans (RRSPs), defined-contribution pension plans, and private-sector defined-benefit pension plans, the CPP builds up no financial assets from which to pay its benefits. It is pay-as-you-go (PAYGO):

the money received by a retiree today is funded, in a straightforward sense, by money paid in by a worker yesterday.

The political advantages of the PAYGO model are clear. Like any Ponzi-style scheme, such as chain letters or multilevel marketing scams, this approach allows large, quick payouts to early participants, whose benefits are paid, not from the proceeds of real investments in plant, equipment, and so on, but from the contributions of the next participant in line[1]. In the mid-1960s, when rapidly rising incomes among younger workers were outpacing those of older workers and retirees whose prime working years had been interrupted by depression and war, such an approach was politically attractive—the first cohort to get full retirement benefits received, on average, annualized returns on their contributions of more than 20 percent, in real terms (Office of the Superintendent of Financial Institutions [OSFI] 1998, 194). Thanks to the unusual circumstances of the postwar years, this approach looked economically viable as well.

The Congenial Environment of the 1960s

The roots of the economic environment of the quarter-century following World War II are still a matter of debate. Technological advances made during the 1930s and the war were transferred into more general use and birthrates rose in the early years of the baby-boom. The 1950s and early 1960s were also characterized by prudent fiscal and monetary policy and a remarkably concerted trade liberalization effort among the advanced democracies. Whatever the causes, 1951 to 1965 was a period of unprecedentedly rapid economic growth and low real interest rates (the growth rate averaged 4.9 percent annually in real terms while long-term government bond yields averaged only 1.6 percentage points over inflation).

This historically unusual situation, with investment returns lower than economic growth rates, made the CPP's unfunded structure look viable. Ponzi games are generally unsustainable because they only work if new funds flow in fast enough to pay previous investors returns better than they could earn with investments in bonds, shares, real estate, and so on. If the inflow of funds shrinks to the point where normal investments become more attractive, the scheme collapses. In the mid-1960s, however, with the prospect of a rapidly growing workforce with rapidly rising incomes on the one hand, and relatively modest returns (at least on "risk-free" government securities) on the other, the Ponzi approach looked viable. A fast-growing tax base would allow supernormal returns even without much increase in contribution rates: in the mid-1960s, the cost of CPP benefits in 2030 was projected at 5.5 percent of covered earnings—not dauntingly higher than the 3.6 percent charged at the start.

Knowing that a pension plan with no money in it might fail to inspire confidence, the plan's designers gave the pyramid a superficially solid look, borrowing the terminology and trappings of regular pension plans. At its base, however, the CPP depended crucially on the indefinite continuation of the economic environment in which it was established.

CRUMBLING FOUNDATIONS

Like the roots of the boom of the 1950s and 1960s, the causes of the slower productivity growth and higher real interest rates that re-emerged after the mid-1970s are still a matter of debate. For someone with a bias toward policy-related explanations, the era that gave rise to the CPP might appear to have contained the seeds of its own destruction. In Canada and abroad, the environment of interest rates lower than growth rates inspired more than unfunded pension plans. It also prompted increases in funded debt and sizeable commitments to ongoing spending in health, education, and welfare—commitments that, in total, presumed a tax-base that would outgrow demographically driven obligations and compound interest.

The End of the Golden Years

Through the later 1970s and into the 1980s, government borrowing in financial markets began to eat into the world's supply of savings, pushing the cost of borrowing up and reducing the resources available for investment in new plants, equipment, and infrastructure. Transfers to the elderly and others grew, further reducing the supply of savings and pushing up the cost of borrowing. As government obligations, funded and unfunded, mounted, the inflation of the 1970s and some notable defaults in the 1980s raised the risk premiums in government debt securities. As obligations became more expensive to service, taxes mounted, further slowing growth.

Whatever the cause, the economic environment that re-emerged at the beginning of the 1980s was one in which, more in line with long-term historical experience, returns on financial assets exceed economic growth rates. Yields on long-term government bonds have averaged 6.4 percentage points over inflation since 1980, while annual real economic growth has averaged only 2.5 percent.

The Problem: Unwilling Recruits

This is not a congenial environment for PAYGO plans. With each actuarial evaluation, the long-term cost of the CPP mounted. By the time of the 15th Actuarial Evaluation, carried out in 1995, the estimated "pay-as-you-go" rate for 2030 had risen from 5.5 percent of covered earnings to 14.2 percent. Worse, the 15th report projected that an inadequate cashflow would exhaust the buffer fund in 2015, and that the subsequent need to replenish it would boost the actual contribution rate to over 15.4 percent in

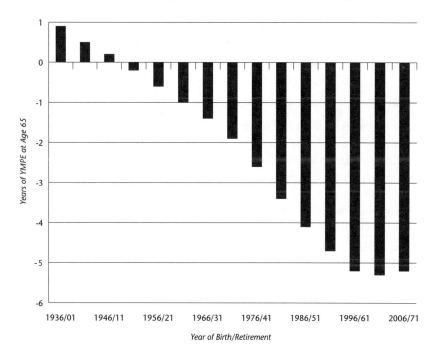

FIGURE 1: **CPP Benefit Gaps by Age, Pre-Reform** (Confident Participants)

Year of Birth/Retirement

2030 (OSFI 1995, 6). Unlike early participants, newer entrants into the CPP were no longer offered an attractive deal.

Compare, for example, the CPP's benefits with the package that the same contributions would provide a typical participant if those contributions were invested in a funded plan. Using data from the 15th Actuarial Report, it is possible to construct a representative CPP participant for whom the present value of money in and money out was typical of a 24-year-old entering full-time work for the first time in 1995 (Robson 1998, 143–43). Before the CPP reforms, what kind of value was this person getting for her/his money? Suppose that the money this person contributed to the CPP had instead gone into a funded plan and earned returns of 4 percent in real terms—a conservative figure, slightly less than the return available (both then and now) on federal real-return bonds. By the time she/he reached age 65 in 2036, she/he would have built up a nest-egg worth about 5.8 times the YMPE for that year[2]. The CPP, by contrast, offered a benefit package that, also valued in 2036 using the same 4 percent real rate, was worth about 3.8 times that year's YMPE.

The difference between the nest-egg and the present value of the benefit package is the cost of CPP participation to this person: a negative "benefit gap" of almost 2 years' worth of covered earnings at retirement. Figure 1 shows benefit gaps for various age cohorts as they stood before the CPP reforms. Although the treatment of a typical participant entering the plan in 1995 was bad, the gap facing later participants was far worse—over 5 years of covered earnings for today's and tomorrow's toddlers.

◼◼◼ THE RISK OF A COLLAPSE

Running an eye across Figure 1 from left to right suggests that time is not on the CPP's side. As the years pass, the number of people who benefit from the CPP is shrinking as a proportion of the total population of voting age, and the number of people for whom the CPP is unattractive is growing.

Skepticism about the CPP's Promises

These circumstances, not unique to Canada, have prompted suggestions for radical reforms of PAYGO systems. Among such reforms, some standard elements are grandparenting existing benefits, covering costs of existing benefits with taxes with broader bases than the existing employer and employee levies, directing future contributions into some sort of funded scheme, and, with varying degrees of severity, scaling back the obligation to current participants who have not yet started receiving benefits. Looking at the changing weights of winners and losers from the CPP in the voting-age population going forward (as in Robson 1996a, 44–48), it is possible to imagine even a relatively severe version of such a plan (such as one in which the plan would default on all obligations not yet in pay) might command a majority in about 20 years' time.

Such calculations are inevitably simpler than what occurs in real life. But a 1994 round-the-world survey of government-run pension plans by the World Bank uncovered not a single example of a plan whose provisions had stayed stable during the time it took for one age cohort to move through it (World Bank 1994, 112). So poll results that show skepticism, particularly among younger age cohorts, about receiving the benefits the CPP promises them have some foundation (Canadian Institute of Actuaries 1995, 18).

Such skepticism matters because, to the degree that participants doubt that the CPP will meet its obligations, the benefit gaps shown in Figure 1— which assume that all obligations would be paid in full—are smaller than they looked to CPP participants. Suppose, somewhat crudely, but in line with polling data, that the expected value of benefits in a participant's eyes shrinks by one percentage point for every year that person is away from age 65. Figure 2 shows the benefit gaps for these skeptical current and future CPP participants before the reforms. For a worker entering the plan in the mid-1990s, a 40 percent reduction in the expected benefits of an unre-

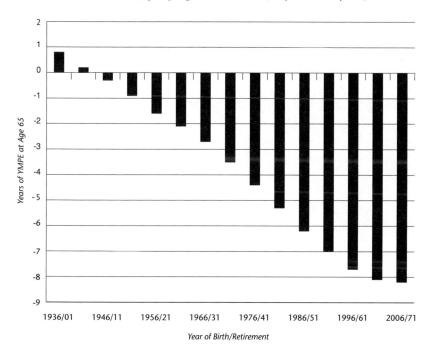

Figure 2: CPP Benefit Gaps by Age, Pre-Reform (Skeptical Participants)

Year of Birth/Retirement

formed CPP would raise the perceived benefit gap of the plan to more than three years of covered earnings at age 65.

The Tax Share of CPP Premiums

These benefit gaps indicate more than intergenerational unfairness. Because they show how much money participants contribute over (or, in the case of older participants, under) what would buy a comparable benefit package in a funded plan, they show how much participants are effectively being taxed (or subsidized). Expressing the benefit gap in relation to the notional nest-egg the premiums would have built in a funded plan yields the share of this person's lifetime premiums that, to him or her, felt like a tax. For example, for the composite participant entering the CPP in the mid-1990s who was confident of receiving his/her benefits, the gap of almost 2 years of YMPE over a total notional nest-egg of almost 6 years of YMPE yields a tax component of lifetime premiums of about one-third. For his/her skeptical counterpart, the tax share is 60 percent. The tax shares of lifetime premiums for various age cohorts of both confident and skeptical participants before the reforms are shown in Figure 3.

The fact that a substantial proportion of the CPP premiums of younger workers feels like tax creates a number of problems. To the extent that

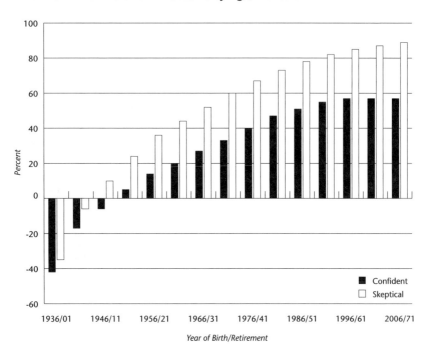

workers see CPP premiums as actuarially fair, providing their money's worth in retirement and other benefits, they will treat them as any other fringe benefit paid for out of their earnings. Rising CPP premiums will be no different from, say, foregoing an increase in base salary for the sake of additional dental plan benefits. To the extent that CPP premiums are a tax, however, the downward adjustment of workers' take-home pay as premiums rise will not be as willingly accepted. For the self-employed, the tax wedge created by CPP premiums discourages additional work for those below the YMPE, and the tax wedge encourages work in the underground economy, or abroad, for all. For employees, to whom the employer-paid half of the levy is less visible, these considerations also apply. For them, however, the passing along of the employer-paid part of the levy in the form of lower wages presents an additional problem. Even if employees are willing to accept the offsetting wage cut (or smaller-than-otherwise wage increase), normal delays in recontracting in the wake of a premium hike will hurt employer cashflow, causing layoffs. And if employees are not willing to accept a wage cut, the passing-along will be slower, making employer cashflow problems more severe and layoffs more widespread.

Money Down the Drain: A Self-Fulfilling Prophecy

The political reaction to premiums that feel largely or mostly like taxes brings the story full circle. Even when asked a tendentious question—"Do you expect to receive: ...more than you put in...about the same amount that you put in...less than you put in"—44 percent of (adult) respondents to a *Maclean's*/CBC year-end poll in 1998 said they expected to do poorly from the CPP (28 percent said they expected to break about even; 22 percent said they expected to do well)[3]. Of those who said they expected less, 38 percent said they were comfortable helping people retiring in the next ten to twenty years to live a better life, while 60 percent (mainly younger respondents and supporters of the Reform and Conservative parties) said they were frustrated by lack of value for their money[4].

To repeat, the passage of time seems sure to increase the share of the population who see the CPP as a poor deal. Even allowing for those willing to accept it for the sake of its redistributive features, suggestions for winding it down will find more sympathetic ears. As more people question the CPP's value, skepticism about benefits will rise, making CPP premiums feel more like a tax, increasing their damage to the economy, and further fueling the political push to do away with the plan in its present form.

■■■ SHORING UP THE PYRAMID

The 1997 Reforms

The release of the 15th Actuarial Report in 1995 prompted fresh interest in the CPP. The most startling news was the plan's dismal cashflow in the early 1990s (due to flagging contributions and a disability-driven explosion of expenditures). The CPP's buffer of funds had started shrinking in 1992, and the existing contribution schedule appeared to be inadequate to keep any funds in the buffer at all past 2015—a projection most frequently summed up in the misleading phrase that the CPP was going bankrupt. As Ottawa and the provinces began the consultative process in preparation for any needed changes to the contribution schedule, they became aware of the depth of skepticism about the plan's durability, and the political will for more far-reaching reforms began developing.

The package that emerged had several elements. It trimmed CPP benefits—a move that was not very significant in quantitative terms, but sent an unprecedented signal that beneficiaries, as well as contributors, bear some of the plan's political risks[5]. It provided for a new arm's-length CPP Investment Board to manage the plan's assets. Most important from a financial point of view, it hiked contributions by freezing the YBE at \$3500 and accelerating the previously planned increase in contribution rates to

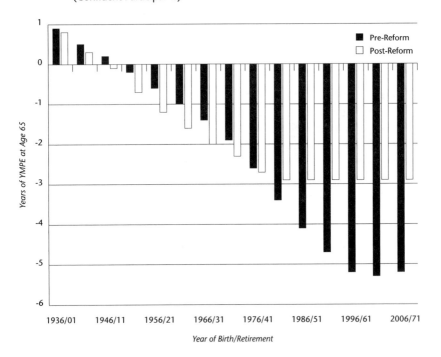

FIGURE 4: CPP Benefit Gaps by Age, Pre- and Post-Reform
(Confident Participants)

Year of Birth/Retirement

reach 9.9 percent of covered earnings by 2003. It also provided for more frequent actuarial evaluations and federal-provincial review of the CPP's condition.

Benefit Gaps Post-Reform

The key thrust of the reforms is to pre-fund more of the obligations that will accrue to CPP participants over the next few years. Instead of turning negative, the plan's buffer is expected to rise to about five years' worth of payouts by 2020, providing more investment income with which to cushion the cost to younger workers of benefits to retiring baby-boomers. As a result, among CPP participants who have full confidence in the plan's promises, the benefit gaps facing current participants are worse than they were before, but the gaps facing future participants are smaller, and never more than about 2 1/2 years of covered earnings (Figure 4).

Based on Figure 4, one might think that the voting-age-weighted balance around the reform package would have been a loser. But many are skeptical about the CPP's durability, and a key intent of the reforms was to boost their confidence. Suppose that the reforms did so—say, halving the discount that participants apply to far-off benefits. In that case, the reform

FIGURE 5: CPP Benefit Gaps by Age, Pre- and Post-Reform
(Skeptical Participants)

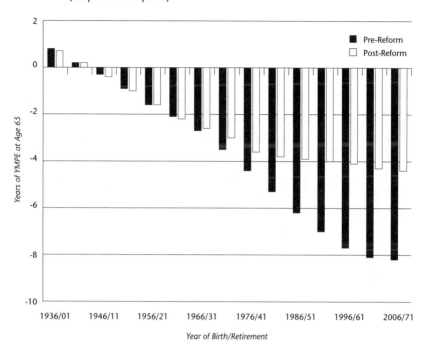

Year of Birth/Retirement

package improved the situation of many current, as well as future, CPP participants (Figure 5).

The Tax Share of CPP Premiums Post-Reform

From an economic point of view, how the reforms impact the share of CPP premiums that participants see as a tax is important. Calculating the tax share by showing the benefit gap as a proportion of the notional nest-egg the premiums have built up outside the plan suggests that the reforms might improve the situation, reducing the amount of their premiums that younger participants consider to be a tax (Figure 6). The improvement in the situation is less than overwhelming, however. Even if my assumption that the reforms halved the skepticism of those who doubt the CPP will endure, a substantial proportion of CPP premiums are still likely to feel much like a tax to those who pay them. And that fact makes the prospect of the higher premiums on the way over the next few years unpleasant.

For example, Peter Dungan has estimated potential impacts of the premium hikes using the FOCUS model at the University of Toronto. One of his investigations looked at two key channels through which the hike could affect output and jobs. One channel was the possible impact of the

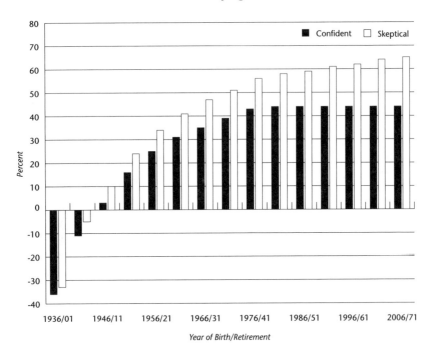

Year of Birth/Retirement

lower take-home pay on work effort (for which he used a labour-supply elasticity of 0.25), which amounts to a scenario in which workers see premiums (or at least the additional amount paid between now and 2003) as all tax. The other channel was the pushing through of the employer-paid portion to employees—a process that presumably will be more painful the likelier employees are to see the levy as conferring no benefit. At its worst in 2003, Dungan estimates that the hike might reduce output some 1.8 percent or $19 billion (in 1996 dollars) from where it otherwise would have been, with a net job loss of 1.6 percent, or 250,000 (Dungan 1998, 14).

It seems reasonable to speculate that costs such as these will be less to the extent that confidence in the CPP's durability increases in the wake of the reforms. Whether confidence will increase or not is, of course, a key and difficult question. On the one hand, the 1997 reforms did trim benefits. Those who are inclined to skepticism have now had a concrete indication that in Canada, as elsewhere, government-run pension plans do not fully honour their obligations. On the other hand, however, the better funding contemplated in the reforms ought to alleviate fears of a massive default. If the projections in the 17th Actuarial Report are borne out, the plan's assets will rise from slightly less than 8 percent of its liabilities at the end of 1997 to slightly over 20 percent of its liabilities in 20 years' time[6]. Since neither of these considerations is likely to be the immediate issue that comes to mind, however, it makes sense to focus on some nearer-term questions in seeking to figure out how people will view the CPP's promises over the next few years.

A MORE STABLE STRUCTURE?

Three features of the current situation rate special notice when it comes to future confidence in, and political support for, the CPP: the activities of the CPP Investment Board, developments during the current federal-provincial review of the CPP's structure, and the apparent durability of the 9.9 percent contribution rate.

The CPP Investment Board

If I were the only judge, the Investment Board would stand out as a positive element in the CPP's future. Its mandate is to give priority to the best interests of the contributors and beneficiaries and strive to achieve a maximum rate of return. The fact that the CPP will continue to be largely unfunded has one positive implication for the Investment Board: not being constrained as funded institutions usually are by the need to match the terms of assets and liabilities and maintain liquidity, the Investment Board has a simpler optimization job to do. And the makeup of the Investment Board's first slate of directors gives no cause for alarm.

This judgement needs tempering, however, with some notes of caution. The record of government-managed social security funds around the world is very poor (World Bank 1994, 27, 28, 95). Even if the CPP Investment Board performs relatively well by international standards, it may still leave much to be desired. The obvious problem is that large pools of money such as these are tempting to governments to use for purposes that would more properly be funded by normal budgetary expenditures—if, that is, they ought to be funded at all. It will be some time before the Investment Board starts coming under pressure to direct its investments according to regional and industrial policy priorities, but it is certain to happen. The fact that the finance minister has already indicated that the 20 percent limit on foreign investment will be "strictly enforced" with regard to the Investment Board's decisions indicates that, in fact, the best interests of CPP participants will not be the sole factor guiding its activities[7].

Most uncertain of all is the degree of public attention that the CPP Investment Board's performance will attract. With the CPP remaining largely unfunded, easily foreseeable annual variations in the performance of its portfolio relative to various benchmarks will be almost immaterial to the security of its benefits. But for much of the public, the small amount of funds actually in the buffer and their use to provide loans to the provinces at below-market rates appear to be key flaws in the current plan. My sense is that political culture in many parts of Canada will be less tolerant of poor performance, particularly when it is connected to politicized fund management, than has been the case in Québec, where this type of arrangement has existed for years. Paradoxically, a better-funded plan may appear less secure in many people's eyes because of occasional, and inevitable, investment losses by the Investment Board.

The Current Review

Also uncertain when it comes to confidence in the CPP, but perhaps likelier to cause mischief, are some issues that were left over after the reform package. As is well known, some provinces and other participants in the reform process had aims inconsistent with the key thrust of the reforms: some liked the CPP the way it was; others, even more Ponzi-like, wanted further benefit enrichment to boost the plan's attractiveness to older participants. Discussions on possible further changes to the CPP are now underway, and some of the items on the agenda—partial pensions for those making a gradual transition to retirement, changes to CPP survivor benefits, and raising the YMPE (Government of Canada 1997)—could raise liabilities and restore some of the tilt against future workers that the reforms removed.

The agreement on the reforms stated that no changes will be considered that would increase the steady-state rate of 9.9 percent. The amended CPP Act further requires that enriched benefits be matched with a temporary contribution rate increase to amortize any unfunded liability they create. The regulation (now awaiting provincial approval) that would manipulate the formula calculating the post-2003 contribution rate shows, however, that these provisions are not as watertight as they might appear.

The Durability of the 9.9 Percent Contribution Rate

The potential inadequacy of the 9.9 percent contribution rate probably presents the greatest risk to future confidence in the CPP. The obvious pricing strategy—inspiring a number just under ten—raised eyebrows when the proposed steady-state rate first appeared in the reform package. But this number seemed important enough to appear in the reform agreement, and the amended CPP Act contains provisions designed to safeguard it—most notably, provisions that if the Chief Actuary finds the rate inadequate and the finance ministers fail to agree on a response, price-indexing of benefits will be frozen in the years 2001, 2002, and 2003 (section 113.(11)). Given the CPP's history of repeated upward adjustments in contribution rates, the unprecedented step of providing for benefit reductions, even temporary ones, signals the importance that designers of the package placed on containing future rate hikes.

**Changes in Steady-State Rate between
16th and 17th Actuarial Reports**

16th Report, after rounding	9.900
16th Report, before rounding	9.923
I. Improvements in methodology	0.037
II. Experience update	
Demographic	0.062
Economic	0.229
Benefits	-0.068
Subtotal	0.223
III. Changes in assumptions	
Fertility	0.279
Migration	-0.492
Mortality	0.318
Disability	0.613
Employment	0.239
Margin of average wage increases over inflation	0.040
Inflation	0.209
Return on investments	0.000
Other (mainly timing of retirement)	-0.300
Subtotal	-0.320
IV. Proposed new calculation method	-0.099
Total of I to IV	-0.159
17th Report rate—before rounding	9.764
17th Report rate—after rounding	9.800

How secure is the 9.9 percent rate? Table 1, adapted from the 17th
Actuarial Report (OSFI 1998, 34), shows how sensitive the calculation of the
steady-state rate is both to developments since the previous report and to
changes in assumptions and forecast methodology[8]. As is typical with actuarial evaluations of the CPP, the experience update is, on balance, negative:
slower growth of the working-age population and worse-than-expected
contributions had put the CPP further in the hole by the end of 1997 than
the previous report had projected. The changes in assumptions are helpful
on balance, however, making the total impact of experience and forecast
updates almost exactly neutral. Before the proposed change in the method
of calculating it, the new steady-state rate would have rounded to be the
same as the old one: 9.9 percent.

It is beyond my competence to go through all the influences on the CPP's future costs in this table and talk about the appropriateness of the assumptions underlying the projection with respect to each. For those who are interested, the report contains both useful discussion of these points and sensitivity tables for the key variables showing how more and less favourable developments than those used in the base projection would affect the results (OSFI 1998, 42)[9]. But one economic variable with which I have considerable familiarity, inflation, gives me cause for concern.

Before the reforms, the ongoing rate of inflation affected the CPP very little, since all of its parameters were fully indexed to either wages or prices. In a manner reminiscent of past federal budgets, however, the reforms changed or removed several indexation provisions to hold the contribution rate down. Some, such as the move to a five-year average of the YMPE for calculating pensions and the freezing of the death benefit at $2500, trim benefits; the most important, the freezing of the YBE, expands the contribution base. Together they mean that inflation, which the previous actuarial report projected at 3.5 percent annually forever, is important in making the package work with a 9.9 percent rate.

Since the Bank of Canada and the Department of Finance have agreed to target a 2 percent inflation rate for the foreseeable future, and average annual Consumer Price Index (CPI) inflation has run half a percentage point below that rate since 1991, the importance of higher inflation in the reform package has long struck me as problematic. The new report confirms this worry. Its inflation projections involve a gradual increase in inflation to an ultimate rate of 3.0 inflation by 2003, rather than the old report's projections of a 3.5 percent ultimate rate starting in 2000. As Table 1 shows, this change raised the steady-state rate by 0.2 percentage points. If the new report had used the Bank/Finance target of 2 percent in its projections instead, the steady-state rate calculation would have come in a further 0.2 percentage points higher, breaching the 9.9 percent ceiling (OSFI 1998, 42)[10].

From my perspective, inflation is a direct and fairly predictable result of the rate of money creation promoted by the Bank of Canada. It is therefore under more direct policy control than any other factor in Table 1. If the actuarial projections foreshadow the future accurately in other respects, and neither the inflation target nor the Bank of Canada's approach to achieving it changes, the 9.9 percent rate will be inadequate.

The change arising from the new proposed method of calculating the steady-state rate gives rise to a different kind of concern. The CPP Act specifies in section 113.1(4) that the steady-state rate should be as low as will result in the CPP's funding ratio "being generally constant..." The designers of the reform package gave effect to this provision by comparing

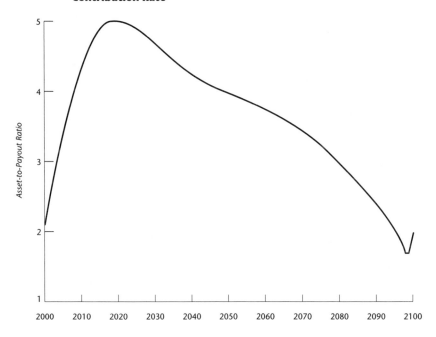

FIGURE 7: **Projected Funding Ratio—2 Percent Inflation and 10 Percent Contribution Rate**

the funding ratio in 2030 and 2100. These years were reasonable: the former because it was late enough for the plan to have reached its target funding ratio; the latter because it was far enough away to ensure that the ratio did not hit the critical value that year while on a steep downward slide. The proposed new regulation, which has yet to receive assent from the required number of provinces[11], would make 2010 and 2060 the reference dates. These years are not reasonable: the funding ratio will be well short of its target in the former year, and the latter is too soon to ensure that, just because the funding ratio is "adequate" in that year, it will still be so in the following years.

The long-term trajectory of the funding ratio with 2 percent inflation and the 10 percent contribution rate after 2002 that goes with it, shown in Figure 7, illustrates the point. In general, using a year well before the funding ratio is expected to peak as the first reference year means that the ratio will be on its way down in the second reference year. In this case, the funding ratio is on a steepening downward track in the second year, and the funds are on their way to exhaustion shortly after the end of the projection period. Describing the rate calculated in this way as "steady-state" is misleading: even if the actual exhaustion of the fund was not projected until after every current CPP participant was dead (and many of their beneficiaries would not be), changes to contribution rates and benefits in anticipation of the event would still affect them.

Since the formal conclusion of the 17th Actuarial Report is that the 9.9 percent steady-state rate is secure even without using the proposed 2010–2060 benchmark, there is little obvious downside for the provinces if they refuse to approve the change. If they do approve it, however—and especially if they do so to create apparent room for plan enrichments being contemplated in the current review—this will be a small but unsettling sign that the long-term stability of the CPP is far from assured.

The Difficulty of Building Confidence

There is clearly more that could be said about the economic and political risks facing the CPP in the coming years. The fundamental point, however, is that the CPP is still, and on current plans will continue to be, more Ponzi game than funded plan. In an environment where investment returns are higher than economic growth rates, the money paid into such a scheme is, for the average participant, partly an unrequited transfer—all the more so to the extent that the participant doubts that the plan will pay its promises in full.

With better funding, sound investments by the CPP Investment Board, resistance to some of the retrograde pressures in the review process, and a mixture of good luck and good management that preserves the 9.9 percent contribution rate, confidence in the CPP may rise. Even the best outcome in these areas, however, will still leave a substantial share of premiums for younger workers effectively a tax, with the job losses and leakage out of the above-ground domestic economy that implies. And in the case of the 9.9 percent contribution rate particularly, the best outcome seems unlikely.

▬▬ LAYING A MORE SOLID FOUNDATION

In a sense, my mandate for this chapter—to discuss the CPP and its problems—runs out here. A general warning about the lack of confidence in the CPP and the added damage premium hikes will do when confidence is low is not, however, a satisfactory note on which to end. Without encroaching unduly on the ground subsequent chapters will cover, therefore, I would like to close with some observations on how we might think about the challenge this situation presents.

More Radical Reforms

If the CPP's problems and lack of public confidence are inherent in its unfunded, Ponzi-style structure, it makes sense to think of more radical reforms that would provide a more fully funded mandatory employment-related pension system and would better insulate its participants from political risks. The broad outlines of one such reform are, as I mentioned earlier, familiar: scaling back and grandparenting existing obligations, financing such obligations with broader-based taxes than the existing payroll-related levies, and directing of some or all of future contributions into accounts controlled largely by the participants themselves. Such a path has been recommended by me and others for Canada (Robson 1996b; Pesando 1997), is being widely adopted in Latin America, and is under discussion in the United States.

Canada's situation is more favourable for such reforms than is often appreciated. For one thing, because Canada already has a well-developed income-support system for the elderly (Old Age Security and the Guaranteed Income Supplement), the safety-net considerations that complicate such reforms in other countries are less pressing here. For another, the broad participation and large sums already in individual and group RRSPs mean that Canada already has much of the necessary regulatory and financial infrastructure. Finally, one of the biggest obstacles to the transition—the need to pay existing obligations and pre-fund accruing ones at the same time—will shrink as the budgetary positions of Ottawa and the provinces improve and funds accumulate in the hands of the CPP Investment Board.

This type of reform strikes many as so radical as to be impossible even if were desirable, but I take encouragement from the speed with which Canada has moved from an official position that all was well five years ago to reforms that make an unprecedented effort to put the CPP on a more solid footing. A move to a new system should be made with comparable speed if we want to avoid some of the job losses that Peter Dungan has warned about and forestall the confidence-destroying efforts to misdirect the funds in the CPP buffer that are sure to come once the Investment Board begins to purchase assets other than non-marketable provincial government bonds.

The Provincial Role

A province has two closely related reasons to look at a separate provincial plan in a situation where confidence in the CPP is shaky and potentially damaging rate hikes are under way.

First, to the citizens of some provinces, though undoubtedly not all, a provincial plan might appear a more reliable guarantee of benefits than the national one. Even the knowledge that such an option existed might enhance confidence, reducing the extent to which CPP premiums feel like a tax to the employees who pay them directly or absorb (in lower take-home pay) the levies paid by their employers.

Second, knowledge that a province is prepared, if necessary, to launch a separate plan might induce better behaviour on the part of other provinces and Ottawa. To the extent that this knowledge helps insulate the CPP Investment Board from pressure to invest inappropriately, forestalls changes to the CPP that would further undermine its stability, or discourages manipulations of calculations related to its financial situation, this move would probably enhance confidence in the plan across the country.

Neither of these benefits would arise if a provincial threat to opt out of the CPP was not credible. As it happens, however, Alberta's relatively young population, its high employment rates and incomes, and its demonstrated desire to run prudent fiscal policies that limit the obligations that today's voters impose on their children and grandchildren make such a threat on Alberta's part credible.

◼◼◼▶ CONCLUSION

To summarize, then, the CPP's predominantly unfunded structure, established during an unusual historical period when it appeared more cost-effective to fund pensions from taxes than from investments, has become a serious liability. The poor deal it offers younger workers has given rise to quite justified fears that it will not meet its obligations in full. Even after the 1997 reform package, the effective tax component of CPP premiums is about 40 percent for those entering the plan in the mid-1990s and after who have full confidence in its benefits, and more than that for those who do not. The tax-like character of CPP premiums for these participants raises familiar concerns about incentives to work in the above-ground economy, in Canada, or at all. This dissatisfaction also intensifies political pressure to slim the plan down, fulfilling the fears of those who doubt its promises.

The fuller funding promised by the recent reform package lessens the CPP's tilt against future workers and ought to enhance confidence in its stability. Especially in the wake of the first actual benefit cuts in the CPP's history, however, there is no guarantee that confidence will actually rise. The mandate and structure of the CPP Investment Board are promising, but the possibility of further changes to the plan and the doubtful durability of the 9.9 percent contribution rate raise concerns for the CPP's outlook. Ironically, confidence in the CPP may be no greater in the wake of the reforms, in which case the passage of time is likely to further erode political support for the plan and increase the damaging effects of the higher premiums now in prospect.

For these reasons, it makes sense to examine further reforms that combine a move toward pre-funded individually controlled retirement accounts with a shift to some other tax base to finance current obligations. Individual provinces can play a role in this process out of proportion to their voting weight in the CPP's amending formula by examining separate pension plans. Such plans could enhance citizens' confidence in receiving promised benefits and could be implemented if other provinces and the federal government do not run the existing plan responsibly. Because of its demographics, economics, and political culture, Alberta seems uniquely well placed to play such a role.

Notes

1. Charles Ponzi was a swindler who launched an arbitrage scheme using U.S. postal-reply coupons in the years immediately following World War I. His initial success attracted overwhelming amounts of money, leading him simply to pass the funds provided by new investors along as dividends to previous ones. The subsequent collapse was so spectacular that his name has been associated with this type of scam ever since. Lest the Ponzi comparison strike defenders of the CPP as objectionable, let me note that Nobel Prize–winning economist Paul Samuelson wrote an article in support of U.S. Social Security in the mid-1960s in which he commented that "a growing nation is the best Ponzi game ever contrived" (Samuelson 1967, 88).

2. Under the 3.5-percent inflation assumption used in the 15th Actuarial Report, the YMPE for 2036 would have been $184,000. The nest-egg built by the accumulated fund in this example would have stood at just over $1 million.

3. Many respondents undoubtedly interpreted the question to mean, Do you think you will get fair value for your money?, but the actual wording is biased, since a relatively small share of participants will actually get fewer dollars out than they put in (Laver 1999, 34).

4. No comparable question, such as Would you be prepared to take slightly less in order to lighten the burden on today's younger workers?, was asked of those who said they expected to get more out than they put in; it is likely that some fraction of that group would say they were willing.

5. The formula for retirement benefits is now based on a five-year average of the YMPE, rather than the previous three, effectively removing one year's wage inflation from the benefit. The maximum death benefit is frozen at $2500. The reforms tightened access to disability benefits and indexed pension entitlements for those disabled prior to retirement to prices rather than wages. They also reduced the maximum benefits available for those receiving combinations of survivor/retirement and survivor/disability benefits.

6. At year-end 1997, the CPP's assets stood at $36.5 billion, and its actuarial liability was $464.5 billion (OSFI 1998, 191). If it were fully funded now, the CPP's assets would be some 25.5 times its annual payouts. Once the baby-boomers are retiring, the fully funded asset/payout ratio would be more like 23 times. Thus by the time the five-times-payouts target is reached around 2020, the plan will be a bit more than 20-percent funded.

7. Pursuing its mandate to serve participants' interests, the CPP Investment Board will, like all such funds, use derivatives to mitigate the impact of the 20-percent rule on its returns. The lack of understanding of investment flows that underlies support for the 20-percent rule may limit the reaction of economic nationalists to this practice. If it becomes an issue, however, and the finance minister responds by trying to restrict the Investment Board's use of such instruments, it would be an ominous sign for the future.

8. The table exaggerates the effect of experience updates between actuarial evaluations slightly because the 16th Actuarial Report, prepared in conjunction with the reform package, took the economic and demographic projections of the previous (the 15th) report as the basis for its projections in order to isolate the effects of the reforms.

9. By its nature, the "other" category of assumptions does not lend itself to sensitivity testing. Since the bulk of the changes in this category relate to assumptions about the timing of retirement, and the CPP's performance is strongly affected by changes in the behaviour of retirees, this omission is unfortunate. With contribution rates rising, many older CPP participants may find the CPP's early retirement provisions more attractive than they otherwise would have, suggesting that reductions in the steady-state rate based on assumptions about later retirement may rest on shaky foundations.

10. It may look odd that the change from the 16th report's 3.5 percent ultimate inflation rate to the 17th report's 3.0 percent rate would raise the steady-state rate by roughly the same amount (0.2 percentage points) as using a 2.0 percent rate in the 17th report would have. The explanation lies in the fact just noted, that the 16th report used the same economic projections as its predecessor. Actual inflation has been, and during the next few years is now projected to be, much lower than the 15th report projected for the 1998–2002 period, cutting into the helpful boost that higher inflation during those years would have given the reformed CPP's finances.

11. As with most CPP provisions, this change requires the assent, through order-in-council, of two-thirds of the participating provinces containing two-thirds of the participating provinces' population.

References

Canadian Institute of Actuaries. 1995. *Troubled Tomorrows: The Report of the Canadian Institute of Actuaries' Task Force on Retirement Savings*. Ottawa: Canadian Institute of Actuaries.

Dungan, Peter. 1998. *The CPP Payroll Tax Hike: Macroeconomic Transition Costs and Alternatives*. C.D. Howe Institute Commentary 116. Toronto: C.D. Howe Institute.

Government of Canada. 1997. *Securing the Canada Pension Plan: Agreement on Proposed Changes to the CPP*. Ottawa.

Laver, Ross. 1999. "To Have and Have Not." *Maclean's* 4 January, 34.

Office of the Superintendent of Financial Institutions (OSFI). 1995. *Canada Pension Plan: Fifteenth Actuarial Report as at 31 December 1993*. Ottawa.

Office of the Superintendent of Financial Institutions (OSFI). 1997. *Canada Pension Plan: Sixteenth Actuarial Report*. Ottawa.

Office of the Superintendent of Financial Institutions (OSFI). 1998. *Canada Pension Plan: Seventeenth Actuarial Report as at 31 December 1997*. Ottawa.

Pesando, James. 1997. *From Tax Grab to Retirement Saving: Privatizing the CPP Premium Hike.* C.D. Howe Institute Commentary 93. Toronto: C.D. Howe Institute.

Robson, William. 1996a. "Ponzi's Pawns: Young Canadians and the Canada Pension Plan." In *When We're 65: Reforming Canada's Retirement Income System,* John Richards and William Watson, eds. Toronto: C.D. Howe Institute.

Robson, William. 1996b. *Putting Some Gold in the Golden Years: Fixing the Canada Pension Plan.* C.D. Howe Institute Commentary 76. Toronto: C.D. Howe Institute.

Robson, William. 1998. "Not as Bad as It Looks: An Intergenerational View of the CPP Tax Hike." In *The 1997 Federal Budget: Retrospect and Prospect,* Thomas Courchene and Thomas Wilson, eds. Kingston: John Deutsch Institute.

Samuelson, Paul. 1967. "Social Security." *Newsweek*, 13 February, 88.

World Bank. 1994. *Averting the Old Age Crisis: Policies to Protect the Old and Promote Growth.* A World Bank Policy Research Project. New York: Oxford University Press.

FRANÇOIS VAILLANCOURT

The Québec Pension Plan

Institutional Arrangements and Lessons for Alberta

THIS CHAPTER DESCRIBES the institutional arrangements of the Québec Pension Plan (QPP) and suggests implications for an Alberta Pension Plan (APP). The QPP should be of interest to those contemplating the pros and cons of an Alberta pension plan, since the QPP is the only subnational public pension plan in North America or among the Organization for Economic Cooperation and Development (OECD) countries. This chapter begins with the institutional setting of the QPP, giving both historical and current information on the two bodies involved in the QPP: the Régie des rentes du Québec (RRQ), which is responsible for collecting pensions and paying benefits, and the Caisse de dépôt et placement du Québec (CDPQ), which is responsible for investing both contributions collected by the RRQ as well as assets of other public bodies. The second part of this chapter draws appropriate lessons for Alberta.

■■■■ THE INSTITUTIONAL SETTING

This section on the institutional setting covers three time periods: first the birth of the QPP, second its evolution over time, and third its current situation (as of 1995/1998, depending on data availability).

The Birth of the QPP, 1960–1965

In the 1960 election campaign, the Québec Liberal Party promised to establish a provincial pension fund to facilitate the transferability of pension funds between employers. Having won the election, the Lesage government set up a committee in late 1961 to examine this issue. This original and somewhat limited goal was, however, affected by the 1962 federal election, in which the promise to nationalize the remaining private electricity utilities was made. Because an implicit alliance existed between the English-speaking owners of the utility companies and Québec's existing borrowing group (led by Ames & Co. and the Bank of Montreal), the Québec government needed to access to new financial capital. With these two goals in mind, by the end of 1962, the Québec model under study was the French "Caisse des dépôts et consignations (CDC)."

In April 1963, the Liberal Party, led by L.B. Pearson, took power in Ottawa. It adopted the plan (first mooted in 1962 by the Diefenbaker government) to set up a Canada pension plan. These simultaneous efforts of both the federal and a provincial government were compatible, since the 1951 amendment to Canada's constitution (then the British North America Act) that allowed the federal government to introduce Old Age Security provided for joint occupancy with provincial paramountcy. One year of federal/provincial discussions followed, culminating on March 31, 1964, by the unveiling of the QPP proposal, which was judged to be more comprehensive than the CPP one. By April 20, Ottawa and Québec agreed to the existence of both the CPP and QPP.

The only unsettled issue was the management of the assets of the QPP: should it be carried out by private fund managers or by a public body? Following a meeting in France between Lesage and the president of the CDC, the decision was taken to set up a public body, whose objectives were set out in a famous speech by Lesage on June 9, 1965. D H Fullerton (1964, 21–34) summarizes the four objectives as follows:

1. to stimulate economic growth in Québec;
2. to manage funds of retirees in a prudent fashion;
3. to widen the market for Québec bonds;
4. to increase the place of francophones in the Québec economy.

Social policy considerations justified creating a public pension plan, while demographic projections indicated that it was viable with the 1996 population of Québec projected (Comité interministériel 1964, Annexe II) to be between 10.8 and 13.7 million (it turned out to be 7.5 million). Differences in the demographic make-up of Canada and Québec in 1961 favoured creating a separate RRQ. The population distribution of Québec, by age group, was as follows: 0–14 years, 35.43 percent; 15–64 years, 58.74 percent; 65+ years, 5.83 percent. In contrast, the rest of Canada (ROC) had the following distribution: 0–14 years, 33.35 percent; 15–64 years, 58.29 percent; 65+ years, 8.36 percent[1]. These differences, however, do not appear to have played an important role, if any, on the decision to originally set up the QPP. Instead, we can conclude that it was mainly the desire to have access to a new source of financing, owned and managed by the Québec government and thus by francophones, that led to the creation of the QPP and, in particular, the CDPQ.

Evolution of the QPP, 1966–1996

To examine the evolution of the RRQ and CDPQ, I present data focusing on the first and last five years (1966–1970 and 1993–1997) as well as for four intermediate years (1975, 1980, 1985, 1990).

TABLE 1: Contributors, Contributions, Pensions, Pensioners and Selected Ratios—RRQ, 1966-1997 (Selected Years)

Québec	1966	1967	1968	1969	1970	1975	1980	1985	1990	1993	1994	1995	1996	1997
1. Contributors[1] (#)	1,950,042	2,054,674	2,080,547	2,138,230	2,181,666	2,669,243	2,865,182	2,897,797	3,174,888	3,045,610	3,071,511	3,054,943	3,109,500	3,157,900
2. % of population 18-69[1]	56.9	58.9	58.7	59.3	59.4	65.3	65.2	62.5	65.1	61.0	61.1	60.4	61.1	61.7
3. Contributions to RRQ (000,000$)[2]	183	225	239	269	281	480	937	1,350	2,336	2,693	2,962	3,186	3,340	3,720
4. % of labour income[2]	1.77	1.98	1.98	2.03	1.95	1.79	1.99	2.00	2.44	2.64	2.83	2.96	n.a.	n.a.
5. % of GDP[3]	1.10	1.25	1.25	1.28	1.25	1.17	1.30	1.26	1.53	1.67	1.77	1.84	1.87	2.0
6. Pensioners (#)[1] Total	n.a.	2,973	15,495	38,534	70,908	212,589	402,705	629,584	851,831	985,926	1,036,426	1,094,833	1,155,649	1,200,786
7. Retirement[1]	n.a.	2,973	10,405	24,015	44,554	115,594	237,039	394,934	562,418	665,671	705,243	754,879	805,630	842,536
8. Survivor[1]	n.a.	n.a.	2,022	6,186	11,768	49,653	100,255	156,107	212,410	243,420	254,239	263,192	272,932	281,479
9. Orphan[1]	n.a.	n.a.	3,068	8,333	14,141	37,238	43,374	38,967	33,917	33,749	32,838	31,377	29,551	28,231
10. Disability[1]	n.a.	n.a.	n.a.	445	445	10,104	22,037	39,576	43,086	43,086	44,106	45,385	47,536	48,540
Retirees as % of older population[1]														
11. 60+[1]	-	-	-	-	-	-	39.5	49.3	54.7	57.1	60.4	62.3	n.a.	n.a.
12. 65+[1]	-	0.8	2.6	5.9	10.5	22.9	39.6	48.4	56.5	60.8	62.4	64.0	66.1	n.a.
13. Pension—RRQ (000,000$)[2]	-	-	4	13	26	194	664	1,841	3,169	4,164	4,439	4,720	4,950	5,190
14. % GDP[3]	-	-	0.02	0.06	0.12	0.47	0.92	1.72	2.07	2.57	2.65	2.73	2.77	2.80

Sources

[1] Régime de rentes du Québec, Statistics Canada, 1996, Tables 6a, 19 and 35 and unpublished data, courtesy of the RRQ, February 1999.

[2] Provincial Economic Account.

[3] Cansim, matrice D (1966-1996) and publication 11-010, Statistics Canada, 1997.

Notes

n.a. Not applicable.

- not available or insignificant.

6 = 7 + 8 + 9 + 10.

11 = 7 (residing in Québec) ÷ population 60+.

12 = 7 (residing in Québec) ÷ population 65+.

The RRQ

As shown in Table 1, the RRQ has seen an increase of about 50 percent in the number of contributors from 1966 to 1995, with an increase in the coverage rate of the population (15+) from 57 percent in 1966 to between 60 and 65 percent. (Greater coverage rates are observed for years of greater economic activity. Since 1993, such rates have been in the 60 to 62 percent range, due to higher unemployment.) The increase in the number of retired pensioners since the plan's inception is much more pronounced. This increase results from the maturing of the regime, the aging of the population, and the decision taken in 1984 to allow payment of a pension to those aged between 60 and 64 (with a 0.5 percent reduction per month of anticipation with respect to age 65). Finally, note that pensioners with retirement benefits represent about 70 percent of all pensioners in 1996.

In terms of financing, contributions to the RRQ increase from 1.1 to 1.8 percent of Québec GDP in 30 years (1966–1995), while pensions go from 0.02 percent in 1968 to 2.73 percent in 1995, with pensions overtaking contributions in the early 1980s. The recently agreed upon increase in CPP/QPP contribution rates, steeper than anticipated a few years ago, will probably lead to contributions higher than pensions in the first few years of the third millennium.

The CDPQ

Tables 2 and 3 present information on the composition of assets administered by the CDPQ and on the importance of various depositors. In regards to assets, from 1966 to 1997, the share of bonds and short-term assets in the portfolio decreased from 100 percent in 1966 to 47 percent in 1997. This end point comparison hides the fact that the share of stocks first increased from 0 in 1966 to 19 percent in 1974, decreased 11 percent from 1975 to 1979, and then increased again. These fluctuations reflect the decisions of various boards and, in particular, the views of the various presidents (both the CDPQ board and president are appointed by the Québec government).

The purchase of stocks by the CDPQ allows it to play an increasing role in the ownership of businesses in Québec and Canada. It is thus interesting to note that, as early as 1971, the CDPQ allied itself with francophone financial institutions to buy out 60 percent of the ownership of National Cablevision (which covered Eastern Montréal, Sherbrooke and Québec City)[2]. In 1979, this ownership position was sold to Videotron, then a startup cable company and now one of Canada's three largest cable companies; the CDPQ financed the Videotron purchase by buying 30 percent of its shares. It is difficult to track the stock ownership of the CDPQ as it began publishing the relevant information only in the 1980s. However, intercorporate ownership information produced by Statistics Canada can provide some indication of its role: as Figure 1 shows, the number of companies

TABLE 2: Assets (000 000$) and Distribution (percent), CDPQ, 1966–1997 (Selected Years)

Assets[1]	1966	1967	1968	1969	1970	1975	1980	1985	1990	1993	1994	1995	1996	1997
Bonds $	153.3	317.3	550.0	735.3	1,004.9	2,577.9	6,485.2	13,703	17,731	22,506	21,345	24,294	25,836	31,001
%	84.79	76.87	81.65	75.34	76.97	70.96	79.79	61.99	49.14	47.52	47.19	46.81	42.75	44.55
Stocks $	0	47.6	99.2	156.6	212.4	638.7	879.4	5,025	12,423	17,782	17,753	20,216	26,073	29,520
%	0	11.53	14.73	16.05	16.27	17.58	10.82	22.76	34.43	37.54	39.25	38.95	43.14	42.42
Mortgages $	0	0	2.7	25.5	44.7	199.0	417.1	1,258	2012	1,958	1,842	1,688	1,567	1,497
%	0	0	0.40	2.61	3.42	5.48	5.13	5.69	5.58	4.13	4.07	3.25	2.59	2.15
Real estate $	0	0	1.1	4.4	14.8	26.1	31.0	318	2,090	2,324	2,294	2,569	3,610	4,281
%	0	0	0.16	0.45	1.13	0.72	0.38	1.44	5.79	4.91	5.07	4.95	5.97	6.15
Short-term assets $	27.6	48.0	20.5	54.2	28.6	191.5	314.7	1,799	1825	2,794	1,995	3,070	2,094	1,618
%	15.27	11.63	3.04	5.55	2.19	5.27	3.87	8.14	5.06	5.90	4.41	5.92	3.47	2.33
Total $	180.8	412.8	673.6	976.0	1,305.6	3,633.1	8,127.4	22,104	36,081	47,364	45,229	51,899	60,432	69,586

Notes

[1] Assets are reported at book value to ensure comparability over time.
In 1996 and 1997, assets also include swap assets (not listed here).

TABLE 3: Deposits (000 000$), CDPQ, 1966–1997 (Selected Years)

Deposits¹ (000,000$)	1966	1967	1968	1969	1970	1975	1980	1985	1990	1993	1994	1995	1996	1997
Depositor														
RRQ	178.5	369.0	618.1	924.7	1,245.2	n.a.	4,548	11,090	14,549	16,401	14,409	15,361	15,660	15,838
CARRA-RREGOP	0	0	0	0	0	n.a.	1,183	4,855	9,970	15,917	16,849	20,441	24,225	27,735
SAAQ	0	0	0	0	0	0	589	2,938	4,836	5,710	4,692	4,974	5,543	6,027
CSST	0	0	0	0	0	n.a.	742	1,944	3,594	4,315	4,219	4,962	5,705	6,883
CCQ	0	0	0	0	0	n.a.	632	1,558	3,013	4,360	4,264	4,943	5,568	6,128
Other							53	12	147	414	427	504	513	1,000
Total						3,567	7,747	22,389	36,259	47,117	44,860	51,185	57,214	63,611
% RRQ in deposits							58.7	49.5	40.4	34.8	32.1	30.0	27.4	24.9

¹　CARRA-RREGOP : Public sector including health and education pension plan (as of 1973).

　SAAQ : Provincial Auto Insurance Plan (personal insurance) (as of 1978).

　CSST : Worker's Compensation Board (as of 1977).

　CCQ : Construction Commission (as of 1970).

n.a. : Not available.

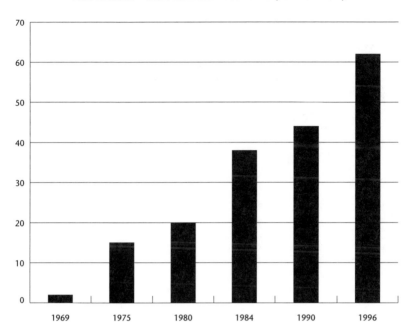

with significant CDPQ stock ownership grew from two in 1969 to sixty-two by 1996. Some of the large shareholdings by the CDPQ in 1996 include Québecor (20 percent), Provigo (36.7 percent), and Videotron (25.2 percent), all firms owned by francophones.

In terms of depositors, the RRQ goes from being the sole depositor to the CDPQ in 1966 (100 percent of deposits), to the largest in 1975 (59 percent), to the second largest in 1994 (32 percent). By 1997, the RRQ only accounts for 25 percent of the deposits to the CDPQ. Since, however, the two pension funds (RRQ and CARRA-RREGOP, the pension fund of public sector employees) account for 68 percent of deposits in 1997, the CDPQ remains mainly a pension fund manager.

The Current QPP (1995+)

The RRQ

In 1997, the RRQ implemented the same changes and, in particular, premium increases, as the CPP. Combined employer-employee rates will go from 6.4 percent in 1998 to 9.9 percent in 2003 and thereafter (increasing by specified increments each year). This rate of 9.9 percent is sustainable in the long-term and replaces the original predicted rate of 13 percent. The

	1996	1997	1998
(1) RRQ (000,000$)	15,761	16,332	n.a.
(2) All pension assets (000,000$)	25,673	34,999	34,228
(3) All assets (000,000$)	52,800	62,374	64,437
(4) % of industry / pension assets	9.6	10.3	8.4
(5) % of industry / total assets	9.8	8.5	7.4

Source: *Benefits Canada, Annual survey, various years, size as of June 30.*

TABLE 5: **Rates of Returns (%), 1995–1998**

	Year 1	Year 3	Year 10
Organization			
CDPQ	13.0	15.6	11.1
OTPPB	15.6	17.5	n.a.
OMERS	14.8	16.1	11.4

Source: *Globe and Mail, November 21, 1998, p. B3.*

Notes: *OTTPB: Ontario's Teachers Public Pension Board.*
OMERS: Ontario's Municipal Employees
Retirement System.

drop of 3.1 percent points is due to the following factors (Régie des rentes du Québec 1997):

1. faster increases in premium (1.0 percent);
2. no indexation of the amount of exempted wages (currently $3,500, which is 10 percent of maximum pensionable earnings) (1.3 percent);
3. use of a five-year average of wages instead of a three-year average to calculate pension benefits (0.4 percent);
4. changes in death benefits and in pensions for disabled workers (0.4 percent).

CDPQ[3]

The CDPQ has enjoyed reasonable rates of returns on each of its portfolios. Management alleges that the overall rate of returns has been reduced because the constraint to hold no more than 40 percent of its portfolio in stocks was lifted in 1997. Tables 4 and 5 present evidence on the size of the CDPQ in recent years and on its rates of returns.

With respect to size, the CDPQ is the largest fund in Canada in terms of pension assets under management for the 1996–1998 period. This reflects, in part, the greater use of outside money managers by other pension funds. (The following top four managers are Philips, Hager and North; RT Capital Management; TAL Investment Council; and Spectre Investment, all private sector firms.) The CDPQ also has real estate affiliates, some of which date back to the mid-1980s (SITQ, Cadim, Ivanhoe, and Cadev). The use of such affiliates appears to be a standard tool of pension funds in the real estate sector. What is more interesting is the creation since 1995 of six specialized affiliates responsible for private investment:

- Capital CDPQ for investment in small firms;
- Capital Amérique for investment in large firms;
- Capital Communication for investment in the communication sector;
- Capital International for investment outside Canada and the United States;
- Sofinov, in partnership with T2C2, for development of new products from university research;
- Services financiers CDPQ for increasing the supply of financial management services in Montréal and the amount thus managed.

The new affiliates were created to regroup the expertise of the CDPQ in these sectors and to allow it to provide seed funding through private investments. CDPQ management argues that this type of investment has higher returns than alternative use of funds. These investments are also more likely to create employment in Québec. Some of these affiliates will, given their mandate, directly complement investment promoting activities of the Québec government. This is particularly the case of Capital Communication and Sofinov. From this perspective, the CDPQ can be seen as an active participant in Québec Inc., whose death may have been prematurely announced. A recent example of this role in Québec Inc. is that, in exchange for tendering its Provigo shares to Loblaws (December 1997), the CDPQ obtained guarantee both that Provigo would continue to purchase the same amount of food products from Québec suppliers/farmers for seven years, and that Provigo would offer its Ontario assets, Loebs (which it is expected to need to sell to satisfy the competition bureau), first to Metro Richelieu, which is Québec's largest supermarket chain and is owned by francophones.

With the birth, history, and current situation of the QPP in mind, I will now focus on three areas from which I believe Alberta can draw lessons. These are: 1) retirement age flexibility; 2) interaction with provincial and federal social programs (specifically as it relates to disability programs); and 3) province-building (as demonstrated through four specific lessons). The first two aspects are RRQ-related, while last aspect and its four lessons are CDPQ-related.

Retirement Age Flexibility

In 1982, the Québec government abolished compulsory retirement, making it illegal to fire someone because of his/her age. This incentive to work longer was counteracted by the introduction in 1984 of the right to receive an actuarially reduced (0.5 percent per month of anticipation) RRQ pension between the ages of 60 and 64 prior to the standard age of retirement, 65. Other provinces also chose to abolish the compulsory age of retirement but did not have the flexibility to encourage early retirement since they were members of the CPP. Indeed, it was only in the late 1980s that the CPP allowed for the receipt of a pension when a person was 60–64. In the future, the RRQ can again be used to modify retirement incentives according to the needs of the Québec population, without the agreement of the other provinces.

■■■■ **LESSON #1**

A provincial universal pension plan along with legislative authority in the pension field gives the province greater flexibility in the retirement aspects of social policy.

Interaction with Federal and Provincial Social Programs: The Issue of Disability

A major increase in the cost of the CPP in recent years has been caused by the increase in disability payments. Interestingly the increase from 1985 onwards in CPP disability recipients is not matched by a similar increase in RRQ disability recipients (see Table 6). Are Québec residents fitter than those of the rest of Canada (ROC), or does the reason lie in inter-governmental financing and interaction in the area of income support programs in Canada?

Table 7 presents the interaction between the four government programs for prime age workers (employment insurance, welfare, disability, and worker's compensation). Provincial welfare programs in ROC will minimize their expenses if they can off-load disabled recipients onto the CPP disability program. They will be particularly interested in doing this when

TABLE 6: **Beneficiaries of CPP-I and RRQ-I, 1970–1994** (Selected Years)

Year	CPP			RRQ		
	Beneficiaries	Contributors	Utilization	Beneficiaries	Contributors	Utilization
	CPP-D	CPP	(%)	RRQ-D	RRQ	(%)
	(1)	(2)	(3)	(4)	(5)	(6)
1970	1,583	6,547,691	-	445	2,176,761	-
1975	46,996	7,421,009	0.63	10,104	2,661,742	0.38
1980	84,795	8,197,717	1.03	22,037	2,856,881	0.77
1985	136,825	8,721,471	1.57	39,576	2,887,827	1.37
1990	202,266	9,603,392	2.11	43,129	3,158,460	1.37
1991	216,603	9,629,629	2.25	43,318	3,166,985	1.37
1992	233,653	9,429,087	2.48	42,810	3,107,061	1.38
1993	258,039	9,399,394	2.75	43,099	3,038,782	1.42
1994	281,190	9,595,358	2.93	44,381	3,071,511	1.44

Source: Vaillancourt, Brule, and Trottier (1997).   *Note:* CPP-D and RRQ-D: disability benefit recipients.

TABLE 7: **Interface between Income Transfer Programs in Canada**

	Employment Insurance (EI)	Welfare	Disability CPP/QPP	Worker's Comp. (WC)
Employment Insurance (EI) (100% F financed)	X	EI benefits expire before reemployment.	Some links for older workers.	Reduced EI benefit makes WC more attractive.
Welfare (1965–1996 : 50/50% F and P financed, with Cap on CAP (1990–1996) and CHST Block grant (1996 +))	Provincial short-term work projects to requalify for EI.	X	ROC: Welfare offices encourage take up of CPP disability to reduce provincial costs.	X
Disability (CPP/QPP : 100% financed by F or Québec)	X	Québec RRQ has tougher disability rules than CPP.	X	X
Worker's Compensation (WC) (100% P financed)	Increased benefits, make EI less attractive.	X	Disability does not require retraining.	X

Source: Vaillancourt (1995), updated.   *Note:* F: federally; P: provincially.

TABLE 8: Observed Growth and Predicted Growth by Factor and Total, CPP-D and RRQ-D, 1983 and 1994

Province	Observed Use and Growth			Predicted Growth Due to				
	1983	1994	(% change)	Unemployment 45–64 Years of Age (% change)	Replacement Rate (% change)	Population 45–64 Years of Age (% change)	Predicted Growth	Predicted Growth/ Observed Growth
	(1)	(2)	(3)	(4)	(5)	(6)	(7)	(8)
Newfoundland	1.76	3.94	123.8	8.4	47.4	33.9	89.7	72.5
Prince Edward Island	1.54	3.20	107.8	14.6	46.3	18.3	79.2	73.5
Nova Scotia	2.90	5.74	97.9	7.2	47.6	16.6	71.4	72.9
New Brunswick	1.91	3.53	84.8	1.1	45.6	20.9	67.6	79.7
Québec	1.09	1.46	33.9	6.2	10.1	17.0	33.3	98.2
Ontario	1.49	3.23	116.8	5.6	36.7	4.1	46.4	39.7
Manitoba	1.15	2.16	87.8	5.1	45.4	3.0	53.5	60.9
Saskatchewan	0.92	2.17	135.9	6.5	48.0	0.8	55.3	40.7
Alberta	0.56	1.75	212.5	13.9	46.4	20.2	80.5	37.9
British Columbia	1.14	2.23	95.6	-0.9	42.9	9.8	51.8	54.2

Sources: *The simulations were carried out using the results of a log-log pooled regression analysis over the 1983–1994 period : the dependent variable is the usage rate . The independent variables are provincial (0, 1) variables, the provincial unemployment rates of the 45–64 age group (three-year average), the provincial wage replacement rates , the provincial share of the 45–64 age group in total population and a (0, 1) variable for the 1987 administrative changes to CPP-D. See Vaillancourt, Brûlé, and Trottier (1997), for details.*

(3) = [(2) ((1) - 1] x 100.

(7) = (4) + (5) + (6).

(8) = (7) ÷ (3).

the federal government provides a reduced share of welfare spending. Because the cap on CAP limited the annual increase in CAP transfers to 5 percent for Ontario, Alberta, and British Columbia, the federal share of welfare spending dropped if total welfare spending grew faster than 5 percent. Although this did not happen in Alberta, it occurred somewhat in British Columbia and significantly in Ontario. In fact, some estimates show Ontario receiving only 25–30 percent federal funding for welfare spending in the early nineties (rather than 50 percent). Québec, however, has an incentive (50/50 funding) to keep the disabled off the RRQ.

Table 8 examines how the caseload of CPP disability evolved by province over the 1983–1994 period and determines if this evolution can be explained by economic factors. The table shows that in Québec the growth in RRQ disability is both the smallest and the best explained by economic factors, while in Ontario the growth is significant and is least explained by economic factors. The introduction of the CHST, a block grant, increases the incentive to use CPP disability since there is no longer 50/50 sharing of welfare costs between the federal and provincial governments in non-capped provinces.

━━━ **LESSON #2**

A province with a provincial universal pension plan faces different incentives than a province participating in the CPP when choosing income support programs for disabled residents.

The CDPQ and Province-building

The CDPQ plays a major role in Québec's economy. It is central to QPP's original goal of giving the government a francophone-controlled source of financing. Therefore, the CDPQ's involvement in the Québec economy could be considered "province-building." I discuss implications arising from four different areas.

1. Local/Francophone Ownership of the Québec Economy

The socioeconomic status of Québec francophones has improved significantly from 1961 to 1991 (Vaillancourt 1996, 69–92). One indicator of this improvement is francophone ownership of the Québec economy, which increased significantly in most sectors (see Table 9). Indeed, among all provinces in 1987, local ownership of the economy is highest in 1987 in Québec, with 68.6 percent of companies' earnings received by companies controlled in Québec, while the percentages for Ontario and Alberta are respectively 58.8 percent and 49.5 percent (Economic Council of Canada 1991). In 1991, foreign control measured by revenue share was 19.7 percent in Québec, 32.7 percent in Ontario, and 26.0 percent in Alberta (Statistics

Sector	Percentage of Total Employment Under											
	Francophone Control (Canadian)				Anglophone Control (Canadian)				Foreign Control			
	1961	1978	1987	1991	1961	1978	1987	1991	1961	1978	1987	1991
Agriculture	91.3	91.8	87.5	97.0	8.7	8.2	12.2	2.3	0¹	0¹	0.3	0.7
Forestry	-²	33.4	92.3	87.7	-²	28.9	7.7	11.3	-²	37.7	0	1.0
Mining	6.5	17.0	35.0	30.0	53.1	18.1	40.4	45.9	40.4	64.9	24.6	24.1
Manufacturing	21.7	27.8	39.3	42.0	47.0	38.6	38.2	33.5	31.3	33.5	22.5	24.5
Construction	50.7	74.4	75.5	86.8	35.2	18.5	21.8	10.1	14.1	7.1	2.7	3.1
Transportation, communications and public services	36.4	42.2	44.9	50.9	55.3	53.4	50.2	44.8	8.3	4.4	4.9	4.3
Commerce	50.4	51.0	57.8	66.1	39.3	32.0	34.0	23.7	11.5	17.0	8.2	10.2
Finance, insurance and real estate	25.8	44.8	58.2	53.7	53.1	43.1	34.6	38.7	21.1	12.1	7.2	7.6
Services	71.4	75.0	75.7	76.8	28.6	21.2	21.6	19.6	0¹	3.8	2.7	3.6
Government	51.8	67.2	67.0	65.2	47.7	32.8	33.0	34.8	0.5	0¹	0¹	0
Total	**47.1**	**54.8**	**61.6**	**65.1**	**39.3**	**31.2**	**30.6**	**26.2**	**13.6**	**13.9**	**7.8**	**8.7**

Source : Vaillancourt and Leblanc (1993, 42–43, Table 3.1)

Notes:

¹By assumption.

²Not calculated. Note that the nature of the data for this sector varies through time in such a manner that interteemporal comparisons are difficult.

Percentage of Francophones in Management Positions in Québec, by Study, 1964–1986

Study	Year	%	Year	%
Secor	1964	69.0	1979	75.0
Sauvé / Champagne	1975	19.3	1981	25.4
Board of Trade	1967	65.6	1979	81.7
Vaillancourt	1971	64.9	1986	77.6
CLF	1977	38.0	1988	58.0

Source: *Vaillancourt (1996).*

Canada 1995). While it is difficult to measure the impact of the CDPQ on this indicator, analysts agree that the CDPQ was an important contributing factor. In particular, it provided support to francophone entrepreneurs: the CDPQ held important blocks of shares that gave francophones effective control of their businesses. Without CDPQ involvement, these entrepreneurs would have needed to own more shares to maintain the same level of control. Local ownership also increases francophone access to managerial jobs, as shown in Table 10.

⬛ LESSON #3

A large public investment pool can be used to increase local control of the economy.

2. Québec's Financial Markets and Specialized Manpower

The CDPQ is the largest trader on the Montreal Stock Exchange, an important purchaser of specialized financial management services from independent firms, and the largest employer of chartered financial analysts in Québec (Canada). In fact, we could consider its primary role to prevent the natural concentration of national financial transactions in one national stock exchange, the TSE. According to this view, the MSE then acts as a regional exchange specialized in small- and medium-sized francophone stocks. Thus, the CDPQ may well reduce the efficiency of Canada's largest financial markets while promoting a smaller market.

In terms of specialized financial services, CDPQ policy encourages Québec firms to provide specialized financial services. In the long term, the policy will create an exportable expertise. (Such an approach replicates Hydro Québec's policy of the 60s and 70s of encouraging the development of world class engineering firms—such as Lavalin and SNC—through its procurement policy.) Finally, the CDPQ is an excellent training ground for specialized financial manpower.

A large public investment fund can be used to help the local financial services industry attain a larger size than it would otherwise.

3. Québec's Government Autonomy

The existence of the CDPQ creates the perception in the market that there is a last resort purchaser of Québec's government bonds (indeed, sometimes the CDPQ does serve as a last resort purchaser of Québec government bonds). This can have an impact on the price of these bonds in times of economic or political tensions, mitigating the market's judgement of provincial politics. (This will be seen as a good result by some and as a bad one by others.)

LESSON #5

A large public investment fund can intervene in the provincial bond market to mitigate the market's judgement of provincial policies.

4. The Governance of Investment Funds

The CDPQ is headed by a director general named by the government for a ten-year mandate, a mandate that can be revoked only by a vote by Québec's national assembly. The CDPQ board is made up of the director general who presides over it; the president of the RRQ (the board's vice-president); nine other voting members, of which at least two are public servants (one is from the union sector and one from the co-op sector); and three non-voting members (the Deputy Minister of Finance, one Hydro Québec representative, and one municipal sector representative). In 1997–1998, the nine other voting members included the president of the two largest unions in Québec (FTQ and CSN), representatives from two depositors (CARRA-RREGOP and SAAQ), and the head of the Caisse Populaire movement. Some nominations to the board reflect the political leanings of the nominees: Marcel Côté was appointed by the Liberals, while Rodrigue Biron was appointed by the Parti Québécois. The administrative structure of the CDPQ first established in 1965 remained unchanged over time from 1990 to 1995, when the positions of president and director general were split.

Obviously then, although the CDPQ is free from day-to-day government interference, the weight its management subscribes to the overall goals of high returns on retirement savings and economic development varies over time. Top management is implicitly expected to accept the relative weights of the current government or to cede its place.

LESSON #6

A large public investment fund can be free from day-to-day government interference but will remain subject to overall public policy directives.

CONCLUSION

As Canada's only separate provincial pension plan, the QPP can provide some insight into a potential APP. The existence of the QPP and in particular of the CDPQ clearly contributes to Québec's greater degree of autonomy in the pension policy area and to an increase in the local ownership of the Québec economy when compared with the alternative of Québec's participation in the CPP. From its birth as an alternative means of government financing, the QPP has grown significantly. The collection and distribution through the RRQ has seen increases so that the RRQ now pays benefits to about 70 percent of Québec's pensioners. The RRQ has also adapted to changing retirement trends. Although the economic impact of CDPQ's investment actions have not been quantified (in GDP per capita), the CDPQ's contributions to the Québec economy have strengthened francophone management and stimulated the growth of Québec's financial sector while providing reasonable rates of returns. Alberta can apply lessons from Québec to gain provincial control of its assets under a separate provincial pension plan.

Notes

1. Interestingly, the differences disappear by 1991, when Québec's share of the population aged 65+ was then at 12.11 percent, almost equal to the rest of Canada's share at 12.17 percent. This population shift can be explained by the drop in fertility, net out-migration between Québec and ROC, and lower (by percent of population) international immigration into Québec than into ROC.
2. National Cablevision's former owners (CBS and Evergreen) had to sell as a result of a federal cabinet decision limiting foreign ownership of cablevision to 20 percent. The CDPQ owned 30 percent of the shares (the maximum statutory participation in its case); the Laurentian insurance company, 25 percent; and two other investors, 5 percent in total.
3. This subsection draws, in part, on the two days of testimony by the Caisse's top management in front of Québec's National Assembly Finance Committee. See "Commission Permanente des finances publiques" (1997).

References

Comité interministériel d'étude sur le Régime des Rentes du Québec. 1964. *Rapport.* Québec: Gouvernment du Québec.

"Commission Permanente des finances publiques—Débats de l'Assemblée Nationale." 1997. CFP 20/21, 3 and 4 September.

Economic Council of Canada. 1991. *28th Annual Report.* Ottawa: Economic Council of Canada.

Fullerton, D.H. 1984. "La Caisse de dépôt—un regard en arrière." In *La Caisse de dépôt et placement au Québec: Sa mission, son impact et sa performance,* C.E. Forget, ed. Toronto: C.D. Howe Institute.

Pelletier, M. 1989. *La machine à milliards: L'histoire de la Caisse de dépôt et placement au Québec.* Montréal: Québec/Amérique.

Régie des rentes du Québec. 1990. *Préparer l'avenir: Histoire de la Régie des rentes du Québec.* Québec: Régie des rentes du Québec.

Régie des rentes du Québec. 1997. "Rapport actuariel modifiant l'analyse actuarielle du Régime des rentes du Québec au 31 décembre 1994." Mimeo. June. Québec: Régie des Rentes du Québec.

Statistics Canada. 1995. *Corporations' Aspects of Foreign Control, Provincial Distribution, 1988–1991.* Ottawa.

Statistics Canada. 1997. CANSIM Matrice D (1966–1996) and publication 11-010. Ottawa.

Vaillancourt, F. 1995. "Income Security in Canada: The Evolving Role of Governments." *Transactions of the Royal Society of Canada,* 6th Series (6), 81–88.

Vaillancourt, F. 1996. "Language and Socioeconomic Status in Québec: Measurement, Findings, Determinants and Policy Costs." *International Journal of the Sociology of Language,* 121 (Special Issue on Economic Approaches to Language and Language Planning), 69–92.

Vaillancourt, F., A. Brûlé, and J. Trottier. 1997. "L'utilisation des programmes d'invalidité du RPC et du RRQ: Une analyse économique." Mimeo. C.R.D.E., Université de Montréal.

Vaillancourt, F. and M. Leblanc. 1993. *La propriété de l'économie du Québec en 1991 selon le groupe d'appartenance linguistique.* Montréal: Office de la langue française.

J.C. HERBERT EMERY &
KENNETH J. McKENZIE

Checking Out of the Hotel California

The Desirability of an Alberta Pension Plan

WITH THE COUNTY MIRED in the midst of its seemingly perpetual self-examination of the state of the federation—as exemplified by the on-going social union talks—it is perhaps appropriate that talk has emerged of Alberta withdrawing from the Canada Pension Plan (CPP) and setting up its own Alberta Pension Plan (APP). Although the public debate has tended to focus on health care, it would appear that all of Canada's social programs, including public pensions, are to be placed under scrutiny as we enter the new millennium.

Talk of an APP has followed closely upon the heels of the recent reforms to the CPP, agreed to in 1997 and implemented January 1, 1999. These reforms were not fundamental in the sense of changing the basic structure of the plan; rather, the hybrid Pay-As-You-Go (PAYGO)/partially funded nature of the plan was maintained. The most important changes involved the expansion of the CPP reserve fund from approximately two years worth of aggregate benefits to five years worth of aggregate benefits. This fund is to be managed by the Canada Pension Plan Investment Board. Unlike the existing fund, it will be invested in "market" instruments rather than provincial government bonds bearing the federal government's borrowing rate. The larger fund is to be built up by accelerating the required increase in the (combined employer-employee) payroll tax contribution rate from 5.6 percent in 1996 to a "steady-state" rate of 9.9 percent by 2003. Without the larger fund, demographic considerations would require a more gradual increase in the payroll tax rate, but would culminate in a much higher 14.2 percent rate by 2030.

Although Alberta, along with seven other provinces, agreed to these changes in the CPP, it would appear that the province did so with some reservations. Alberta Premier Ralph Klein indicated at the Progressive Conservative convention in October 1997 that this move "was deemed at the time to be making the best of a bad situation, to make the fund whole and pure again" (*Alberta Report* 17 November 1997). The delegates to that same PC convention asked the premier to investigate taking Alberta out of

41

the CPP and starting an APP. In response, Alberta Treasury under Treasurer Stockwell Day is apparently considering seven or eight different kinds of plans (*Alberta Report* 17 November 1997).

There has been a great deal of discussion, in Canada and elsewhere, regarding the reform of contributory public pensions such as the CPP. Most of the debate has concerned the merits of the PAYGO approach versus a fully funded system, and, in the case of the latter, whether a privately or publicly managed system is preferred. Recently, an emerging discussion on the reforms of public pensions has focused on the merits of a sub-nationally administered contributory pension plan. To our knowledge, most of the recent discussion has been presented in the media, with little or no analytical work to back it up. This chapter makes an initial foray into this area by examining the merits of a separate APP.

This is a daunting task for several reasons. One of the most significant problems we face in analyzing the replacement of the CPP with an APP is the ultimate form the APP may take. Will it be similar in form and structure to the CPP (that is, PAYGO with partial funding)? Or will the APP be a completely different form (such as a fully funded defined benefit program or a "privatized" mandatory defined contribution program)? A related issue concerns the terms and conditions under which Alberta could withdraw from the CPP

We deal with these issues as follows. We largely ignore the latter, and simply presume that an arrangement could be worked out. Nonetheless, we make some assumptions about how Alberta and Canada will deal with the CPP entitlements of currently retired and working Albertans. The only constraint we impose in this regard is that the APP must provide "comparable benefits" to the CPP, as required by the Canada Pension Plan Act. Of course these "comparable benefits" can be provided by various sorts of plans, which brings us to the first issue of what an APP might look like. Although Alberta Treasury is apparently considering multiple types of plans, we have neither the time nor resources to consider many different alternatives. Rather, we consider two broad possibilities. The first assumes that the APP mimics the general structure of the CPP (PAYGO with partial funding). We analyze this scenario in some detail. The second scenario assumes that the APP is a radical departure from the PAYGO concept. In particular, we assume that Alberta moves to a fully funded approach. Given time and data constraints, our analysis of this scenario is less detailed and more tentative. In the next chapter, Robert Brown deals with this case in more detail.

Canada already has some experience with a sub-nationally managed pension plan that co-exists with the CPP—the Québec Pension Plan (QPP). In the next section we very briefly consider the history of contributory public pensions in Canada, paying particular attention to the QPP. This, we think, provides some important context and allows us to introduce some issues that arise in connection with an APP that did not arise in the case of the QPP. Next we present some of the possible arguments that have been made in support of a separate APP. These include demographic differences between Alberta and the rest of the country. We analyze a PAYGO APP alternative in light of these considerations. In the last section, we briefly consider some of the issues that may arise in the case of a more radical departure from the CPP in the form of a fully funded APP.

⬛ LESSONS FROM THE PAST: THE ORIGINS OF THE CPP AND QPP

The interest in a separate provincial pension plan for Alberta as an alternative to the existing "national" plan is reminiscent in many ways of the origins of the CPP. Particularly relevant in this regard is the role played by provinces interested in having their own contributory pension programs. A brief examination of the origins of the CPP and QPP provides us with some useful insights in our consideration of the merits of an APP.

At the time that Diefenbaker's Conservative government (and subsequently Pearson's Liberal government) was considering the introduction of a national contributory pension plan, Ontario and Québec were investigating the possibility of their own provincial contributory pension plans. In the end, Ontario abandoned its plan and entered into the federal government's CPP, while Québec went ahead with its own plan, and along the way helped shape the CPP. (It is important to note that pensions and care for the aged were initially under provincial, not federal, jurisdiction.) Further, the CPP's initial design offered provinces the right to use/borrow— at the federal government's borrowing rate—excess CPP funds generated in their province for their own purposes. Provinces were also given the option of administering the plan themselves according to the federal parameters or leaving the administration to the federal government. Ultimately the nine anglophone provinces chose administration by the federal government. Today, with the notable exception of the QPP, public pensions are administered entirely by the federal government. Nonetheless, public pensions remain a shared responsibility under the constitution—the CPP is reviewed every five years with a requirement that any changes be agreed to by two-thirds of the provinces representing at least two-thirds of the population.

When the federal government sought initially to implement pensions/ income support for the elderly in the late 1940s and early 1950s, there was some ambiguity as to whether the federal government had the right to set up a pension plan. While the British North America Act (BNA Act) failed to specify whether income support for the aged was a federal or provincial responsibility, legal opinion held that pensions for the elderly fell primarily under provincial jurisdiction. While there was clearly a role for federal participation in non-contributory public pensions, it was commonly held that the federal government did not have exclusive, nor even primary, legislative jurisdiction in this regard.

With the exception of Québec, from as early as the 1920s the provinces showed little interest in developing policies on public pensions and made little or no attempt to keep the federal government out of that area of provincial legislative dominion. Kenneth Bryden suggests that this reflected the popular perception that pension plans were fulfilling "a national purpose"(1974, 201). With the federal pension act of 1927 and through the 1940s and 1950s, the provinces (with the exception of Québec) made no attempt to defend their jurisdiction over pensions. In 1950 the anglophone provinces welcomed the federal assumption of exclusive responsibility for a universal pension plan and later agreed to a constitutional amendment to enable Ottawa to impose earmarked taxes to finance it. In 1951 the insertion of Section 94a into the BNA Act recognized that both levels of government had the legislative right to provide old age pensions. Federal legislation on pensions, however, would remain secondary to provincial initiatives. Even with the 1951 constitutional amendment, federal legislation relating to old age benefits would be inoperative in any province where comparable provincial legislation existed.

It is not entirely clear why the provinces (other than Québec) so readily allowed the federal government to assume the primary responsibility for pension legislation. Bryden suggests that the provinces had concerns over the containment of pension costs and preferred to leave that headache to the federal government. He also suggests that, other than Québec, the other nine provinces were satisfied with the federal government's exercise over jurisdiction in the area of family allowances and unemployment insurance. By the early 1960s they were similarly satisfied with the federal government's handling of universal old age pensions. Thus, as the CPP was being designed in the early 1960s and administered after 1965, the provinces had no reason not to yield jurisdiction to the federal government.

The precursor to the CPP was the non-contributory universal pension benefit that had existed since 1951. Enriching the existing benefit was considered to be undesirable because of concerns regarding the curtailment of costs. A contributory, or earnings-related, pension plan, where an individual's benefits would be directly related to the amount of his/her contributions was seen as a solution. If Canadians desired a larger pension, they would have to pay more and they would recognize this in a contributory program. By the early 1960s the federal government was actively investigating the feasibility and details of such a contributory pension program. At the same time, Ontario and Québec were also investigating setting up their own contributory pension programs. Ontario's plan, ultimately abandoned, was less comprehensive than Ottawa's; Québec's plan was more comprehensive than Ottawa's.

Québec's earnings-related pension plan (ultimately the QPP) fundamentally affected the design of the CPP that was implemented in the other nine provinces. Diefenbaker's (and later Pearson's) government envisioned a national contributory pension plan and thus wanted Québec to participate. At the same time, Québec was aggressively embarking on a campaign to eliminate the power of the federal government in Québec:

> The new government (of Québec) wanted a well-developed social security system, but it was to be a Québec system devised by Québecois for Québecois. This position did not apply only to shared-cost programs. It applied equally to three major areas—unemployment insurance, family allowances and universal old age pensions—where the federal government had been exercising exclusive jurisdiction for years, to the satisfaction of the other provinces. In the case of the universal pension, Lesage presented a claim at the federal-provincial conference of July 26–27, 1963, for federal withdrawal in Québec, with financial compensation through removal of the old age security tax in the province or payment of a fiscal equivalent. Constitutionally, the province could probably have preempted the field simply by putting in a universal plan of its own into operation. This was rendered impractical, however, by the fact that the federal government was levying taxes in Québec which were ear-marked for the national plan. The Québec government wanted a free hand to develop a complete old age security program conforming to its own assessment of the needs of the aged in the context of the total social security requirements of the province. (Bryden 1974, 163–164)

In this sense, the origins of the QPP had more to do with province-building, political and cultural influences than fiscal concerns. It is interesting (and relevant) to note that Québec's implementation of its own contributory plan was initially stalled by the existence of transition costs. In particular, Québec faced the possibility that withdrawing from the federal pension program would disqualify Québecers from receiving federal benefits, yet leave them still paying into the federal system. What improved Québec's bargaining position was Diefenbaker's insistence that the federal contributory pension plan include survivor's and disability benefits. As the 1951 amendment to the BNA Act dealt with old age pensions and not these other benefits, the federal government required an additional constitutional amendment to include them. In 1963 Québec offered to agree to a constitutional amendment of Section 94a of the BNA Act that would allow the federal government to include survivor's and disability benefits in its earnings-related pension program. In return, Québec had "the express condition that the text thus modified includes for each province (insofar as old age security, aid to widows, orphans and invalids are concerned) the option of withdrawing completely from the federal program with full financial compensation" (Bryden 1974, 168). The federal government did not agree to this condition. They continued negotiations with the Québec government and a compromise was agreed upon in 1965. The compromise gave Québec its own plan, but Québec and Ottawa's plans would be identical in terms of coverage, eligibility, contributions, benefits, and funding. Québec assented to the constitutional amendment to allow the federal government to include survivor's and disability benefits without the "opting out with compensation" condition.

As part of the province-building focus, the Québec pension plan called for the accumulation of a reserve fund out of which government investments in "social capital" would be made. In contrast, the Ottawa plan in 1963 called for no reserve fund since such a fund was widely recognized as unnecessary in a PAYGO plan, the solvency of which is guaranteed by the government's ability to tax. By 1965, Ottawa's attempts to get Québec to participate in a national plan yielded a compromise that created a small reserve fund for the federal plan and allowed Québec to generate its own larger reserve fund. As the compromise also called for the same level of benefits and contribution rates across the two programs (to ensure inter-plan portability of benefits) Québec accumulated the larger fund by selecting a transition period of 20 years for the payment of benefits, versus only 10 years for the federal plan. Bryden (1974, 169) concludes that "Québec asserted successfully the paramouncy of its jurisdiction, while Ottawa was able to hold out the prospect that the terms, if not the administration, of the new formulation would be nationwide in application."

Following the compromise, there was a need to put the other provinces on the same footing as Québec. To do this, Pearson offered the nine anglophone provinces the option of either administering the common plan themselves or, if they chose federal administration, of receiving all the investment funds generated by contributions in their territories.

Ontario was not enamoured of the federal-Québec compromise. Ontario's dissent had less to do with the details of the plan and more to do with the view that the government's involvement in pensions should be less, not more. Once Ottawa decided to go ahead with its plan, Ontario's only choice was to accept the federal-Québec plan in full, with federal administration, or implement its own comprehensive plan to render the federal legislation inoperative in Ontario[1]. In the end, political logic (an oxymoron, of course) dictated that the federal plan with federal administration was the only choice. As Bryden describes it:

> If, on the one hand, the terms of an Ontario plan were substantially different from Ottawa's, the provincial government would suffer the opprobrium of excluding its constituents from the nationwide portability which apparently had been achieved by the federal-Québec settlement. On the other hand, if the terms were identical, the [Ontario] government would have a difficult task of explaining why provincial administration was necessary. The difficulty would be compounded by the fact that entirely new machinery would have to be established to collect necessary contributions, a problem not encountered in Québec as it had been collecting its own income tax since 1954 and pension contributions could be integrated with that collection. A public opinion poll published in July, 1964, indicated that most respondents outside Québec favoured federal administration. (Bryden 1974, 174)

In the end, Québec's cultural individuality and administrative infrastructure made a separate, yet similar, QPP a realistic option. In Ontario, and in the other anglophone provinces, the desire for provincial control *vis-à-vis* federal control did not exist, nor did the administrative infrastructure. In this regard, provincial plans outside of Québec had little support politically and did not make sense financially. The province-building motive was just not as strong in the other provinces.

Perhaps Ontario's conundrum in the 1960s is the best illustration of the difficulties Alberta might face in "going it alone." First, the negative demographic shock an Alberta withdrawal would impose on the CPP is similar to the negative tax base shock Ontario's non-participation in the federal plan would have imposed. One might expect that Ottawa would work hard to avoid this outcome. Second, there is legitimate concern over portability of benefits if Alberta were to implement an APP that differed too much from the surviving CPP. On the other hand, an APP identical to the CPP may be sold on the grounds that this would allow the Alberta government to control the pension fund. The benefits, if any, of having the fund under provincial government control must be balanced against the costs of setting up the administrative machinery to operate a separate APP. Indeed, one view is that Alberta may be better off threatening to leave the CPP to get the federal government to turn over CPP investment funds generated in Alberta to the province, as Pearson promised in 1965, but to have the federal government continue to administer the CPP in Alberta. This is not an approach we necessarily advocate.

We can also compare Alberta to the Québec of the 1960s. Similar to Québec, Alberta seems to desire to wrest control of the pension funds generated in Alberta from the federal government. If Québec can run a pension plan separate from the rest of the country, why can't Alberta?

We emphasize two considerations: the first is that the QPP very closely mimics the CPP; the second is that the QPP is not, in our view, an appropriate model for an APP. When the QPP was established, Québec had the tax infrastructure in place to operate its own plan. (Alberta does not.) Moreover Québec was able to direct the design of the CPP to ensure their participation. And, perhaps most importantly, when the QPP was established there were no transition costs, since it was introduced in conjunction with the CPP and did not involve a switch from an existing contributory pension program. The provinces in the 1960s had little trouble entering into a contributory pension program, as there were no accumulated entitlements. Now, however, Albertans must be concerned about the security of their CPP entitlements should they withdraw from the CPP. Thus, now that the entitlements have accumulated and transition costs have increased, a province may never really leave the plan, at least with a clean slate. As our title suggests, in this sense the CPP for the provinces is much like the Eagles' song, "Hotel California"—you can check out anytime you want, but you can never really leave.

▄▄▄ WHY A SEPARATE APP?

Nonetheless, many Albertans still think a separate APP is worth investigating. In this section we present three reasons often given in support of a separate APP.

In the previous section we alluded to some reasons that caused Québec to pursue a separate QPP in 1966. Certain of these reasons may well ring loudly in Alberta, at least for some. For example, one possible motivation for seeking a separate APP is to gain control of Alberta's share of the pension fund, allowing the province to invest the fund as it sees fit. As discussed above, this was an issue at the inception of the CPP. The idea that an APP would give Albertans control of the fund is reminiscent of the province-building motive for the QPP discussed earlier. (François Vaillancourt discusses this issue from the perspective of Québec in the previous chapter.) While it would be foolish to completely ignore these sentiments in an Alberta context, we do not find the arguments convincing. Two points are relevant here. First, as the previous section suggests, it appears possible for the Alberta government to gain control of its share of the fund within the context of the current CPP. Indeed, this opportunity was offered to the provinces at the inception of the CPP. Second, the potential politicization of the fund if this were to occur is worrisome and problematic for obvious reasons. These concerns exist for the larger CPP fund at the federal level, and speak to the political independence of the new Canada Pension Plan Investment Board. These issues would clearly exist for Alberta, and may be more pronounced at the provincial level.

Another possible motivation for seeking a separate APP arises from differences in the demographics and the labour force participation rates of Alberta's population *vis-à-vis* the rest of Canada's population. These considerations may suggest that even if the APP maintains the basic structure of the CPP (PAYGO with partial funding), Albertans may be better off with their own plan. This appears to be the most common reason cited for Alberta going it alone, and we will soon deal with it at length.

A third reason why a separate APP may be desirable is that it may allow the province to adopt a completely different approach to contributory pensions. This is typically thought to involve some sort of fully funded approach. We discuss this alternative briefly in the next section; Robert Brown gives it more attention in the next chapter. Related to this argument is "the thin edge of the wedge" argument. The idea here is that if Alberta moves to some sort of fully funded pension, then the rest of the country may follow. This seems to be the argument made by Robson in his contribution to this volume. This argument is attractive if you believe that fully funded contributory public pension plans are desirable (as Robson clearly does) and if you believe that Canada will inevitably follow (which is open to question). It is also consistent with the view that one advantage of the decentralization of social programs, including pensions, is that it fosters experimentation if not outright competition in social policy, which can be beneficial.

Our response to these arguments is two-fold. First, our intention in this chapter is not to take up the argument as to whether a fully funded or PAYGO system is more appropriate. Many others have addressed this issue—and Brown does it admirably in his chapter—and our contribution in this regard would be minimal. We attempt the difficult task of separating the issue of pension design from the issue of decentralization, focusing primarily on the latter. Second, while we agree with the idea that decentralization can indeed foster experimentation and competition, we must also recognize the costs of this competition. Duplicate administrative structures, risk pooling, portability, and transition costs are all considerations that we deal with below. Another issue is the possibility of "destructive competition." Many have questioned the sustainability of decentrally designed and managed social programs in the face of a mobile population. While these questions tend to arise more in connection with income redistribution programs, some of the arguments are relevant here as well. In particular, if social programs begin to vary drastically across provinces, "fiscally induced migration" may introduce inefficiencies into the labour

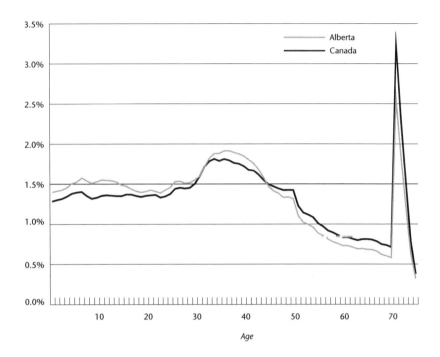

Age

market; again, we will discuss this in more detail below. If a fully funded contributory pension is desirable, then our view is that this would be best accomplished on a national scale rather than a provincial one.

The Demographic Advantage in Alberta

Now we consider in more detail the second reason for a separate APP: Alberta's demographic advantage. Alberta has a younger population than the rest of Canada, though the differences in the age distributions are not as pronounced as commonly perceived. The mean and median age in Alberta is 33 compared to 35 for all of Canada. Fifty-five percent of Alberta's population is between the ages of 16 and 50, compared to 53.4 percent of Canada's population. Figure 1 and Table 1 show the age distribution in Alberta and Canada as a whole (including Alberta) for 1996. Of particular note in Figure 1 is the substantial demographic bulge in Alberta relative to the rest of the country in the 35–50 age group, and, to a lesser extent, the presence of relatively fewer people over 50.

Age Range	Percentage of Total Population, Alberta	Percentage of Total Population, Canada
15 and under	22.5	20.2
16 through 24	14.2	13.6
24 through 44	34.3	32.9
45 through 64	19.2	21.3
65 and older	9.8	12.0

Source: Statistics Canada CANISM Matrices 6367, 6376.

Although revealing, these age distributions are somewhat misleading as they are expressed over the entire population, working and non-working. For purposes of analyzing contributory public pensions, we are more interested in the working population, as this is the population that pays into the CPP and is entitled to CPP benefits. This is particularly important if the labour force participation rates for the various age groups are different in Alberta than the rest of the country. Figure 2 presents the adjusted demographic distribution between ages 18 and 64 accounting for differences in the labour force participation rate.

Comparing Figure 2 to Figure 1 over the relevant age groups, note that the age distribution of Alberta has shifted up relative to Canada's age distribution. Alberta's demographic bulge in the 35–50 group is more pronounced than in Figure 1. Accounting for participation also renders the proportion of the working population over 50 roughly the same in Alberta and Canada as a whole. This arises from the fact that the labour force participation rate in Alberta is higher than the rest of the country at every age group. This, of course, means that there is not only a greater proportion of the entire population paying into the plan, but that a greater proportion of the population will be entitled to benefits.

Another reason that these population numbers may slightly overstate an Alberta demographic advantage is the issue of residency. With a national pension program, the residency of retired Canadians is irrelevant. With a provincial pension plan with portability of benefits, the relevant retired population is not only those Albertans retired in Alberta but also retired Albertans living in other provinces (such as British Columbia).

"Alberta is getting hosed..."
The challenge that remains is to determine the extent to which Alberta's demographic advantage may translate into a tangible benefit under a sepa-

Figure 2: Percentage of Population Participating in Labour Force, Alberta and Canada, 1996

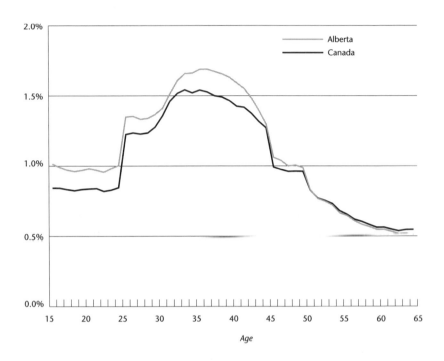

Age

rate APP. A popular way of quantifying this advantage has been to focus on the net flows of CPP revenues and expenditures between provinces. Not surprisingly, these numbers show that there is a substantial net outflow of CPP contributions from Alberta.

Alberta's younger population coupled with the PAYGO nature of the CPP suggests that as a group Albertans contribute more to the CPP than they receive. In 1996, for example, Albertans paid $2.087 billion into the CPP and received $1.643 billion in benefits, for a net outflow of $444 million[2]. Indeed, Alberta is the only province in the country with contributions exceeding benefits. Figure 3 shows CPP contribution per dollar of benefits received for each province and the country as a whole for 1996. In 1996 Albertans paid $1.27 per dollar of benefits received, while Canadians overall paid 92 cents. The fact that the country as a whole was running a deficit on the CPP account in 1996 is, of course, reflective of the problems with the plan that necessitated the changes agreed to in 1997. British Columbia and Saskatchewan have the lowest ratio of contributions to benefits, at about 80 cents. This reflects the relatively high proportion of retired individuals in these two provinces[3].

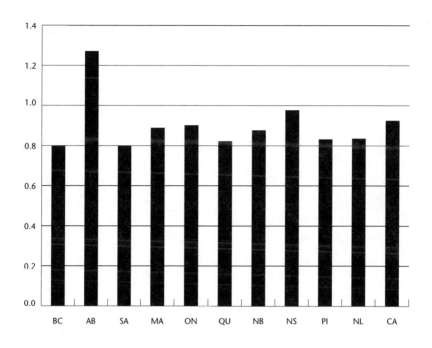

Figure 4 shows CPP contributions per dollar of benefits for Alberta from 1992 to 1996. This figure shows that there has been a fairly steady decline in the ratio, from a high of $1.43 in 1992 to the current level of $1.27. This is notable for two reasons. First, it reflects that fact that although Alberta continues to have a demographic "advantage" over the rest of the country, that advantage has eroded somewhat. This is likely to continue as the demographic bulge in the 35–50 year range (see Figures 1 and 2) ages and moves into retirement. This is an important issue to which we return below. Second, it emphasizes that net CPP flows can change substantially from year to year, and it may therefore be misleading to look at an individual year.

The net outflow of CPP contributions over benefits in Alberta, which was $444 million in 1996, seems to be the source of most of the consternation regarding Alberta's role in the CPP. Indeed, this outflow promoted University of Calgary political scientist Tom Flanagan to comment in a recent interview that "Alberta is getting hosed" (*Globe and Mail* 6 November 1997, A27). Flanagan went on to point out that fewer people in Alberta receive employment insurance (EI) and welfare, implying that the

FIGURE 4: CPP Contributions per Dollar of Benefit Paid: Alberta 1992–1996

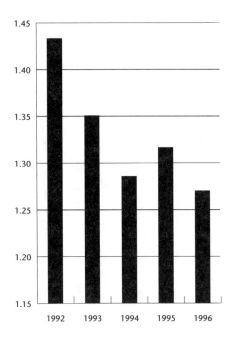

net outflow of CPP contributions from Alberta is just part of a much bigger outflow problem. In other words, the not so implicit implication is that Albertans are subsidizing the other provinces through the CPP (and EI) system.

While we cannot quibble with the conclusion that there is, and has been, a substantial net outflow of both CPP and EI contributions from Alberta, we think that the analogy between regional CPP outflows and EI transfers is flawed. EI transfers are affected by differences in unemployment risk across industries and the failure to use actuarial principles in setting EI premiums. Insurance/actuarial principles suggest that high risk industries, and/or the individuals working in those industries, should have higher EI premiums than low risk industries. This is referred to as experience rating. To the extent that premiums do not reflect these differences—and in Canada they do not because our EI system is flat rated (or even negatively experience rated in some respects)—premiums paid by low risk industries, and the workers in those industries, effectively subsidize high risk industries. To the extent that high risk industries are located in particular provinces, unemployment risk and the degree of implicit subsidy offered by the EI system will differ by region. In this sense, it is legitimate to characterize net EI inflows into different provinces as reflective of an implicit regional subsidy. The same interpretation cannot be made for the CPP. Unlike EI, where the probability of unemployment (and therefore the possibility of receiving EI benefits) may change markedly when an individual changes provinces, CPP benefits are attached to the individual—they are the same no matter where the individual may reside. CPP transfers (subsidies) are intergenerational, not interregional.

Our somewhat obvious point is that differences in net EI contributions across regions can be thought to legitimately reflect interregional subsidies associated with different unemployment risks across regions and industries. Differences in net CPP contributions across regions should not be similarly interpreted, as they are reflective of intergenerational subsidies, not interregional subsidies. A thirty year old working in Ontario pays the same intergenerational subsidy as a thirty year old working in Alberta. It is not so much that Alberta is "getting hosed" as it is that younger workers, regardless of where they live, are getting hosed.

The intergenerational transfers associated with a PAYGO pension can be seen by calculating what are called "Lifetime Cost Benefit Ratios" (LCBR) associated with the CPP for Canadians of different ages. The LCBRs are the ratio of the net present value (NPV) of lifetime CPP contributions to the net present value of lifetime benefits. A ratio of 1.0 indicates that the NPV of benefits equals the NPV of lifetime contributions. In other words, a contributor breaks even. The LCBR of a fully funded pension plan is 1.0. An LCBR of greater than one indicates that the NPV of benefits is less than the NPV of contributions (and vice versa). Philip Oreopolous (1996) has undertaken LCBR calculations for the CPP. His calculations suggest that Canadians under 50 will receive less in benefits than they pay into the CPP (in present value terms). Thus, for many Canadians, the CPP in its PAYGO format is not the best means of securing retirement income.

If we weight Oreopolous' age-specific LCBRs by the percentage of the population who face those LCBRs we can determine the "average" LCBR for Canada and Alberta[4]. As discussed above, it is important to note that population does not equal the employed work force who actually contribute to the CPP (which incorporates participation and employment status) but it allows us to characterize differences between Alberta and Canada with regards to the CPP.

First we use Oreopolous' age-specific LCBRs calculated under the scenario that the CPP remains PAYGO and premiums rise to 14.2 percent over 30 years. This situation represents what would have happened with the CPP in the absence of federal government's changes to the CPP implemented in January 1999. The average LCBR is 1.49 for Alberta versus 1.42 for Canada. Because Alberta's population is younger, and a larger portion of it will be paying the higher premiums (and receiving benefits further in the future), the CPP is a poorer paying proposition for the *average* Albertan, than for the *average* Canadian. But, again, it is important to realize that an Albertan and Ontarian of the same age (and wage) have the same LCBR, so this difference reflects compositional differences in population, not differential treatment across provinces.

Second, calculating Oreopolous' age-specific LCBRs under the scenario that CPP payroll taxes rise to 10.8 percent over the next 7 years yields an Alberta LCBR of 1.51 versus 1.45 for Canada. This scenario closely resembles that implemented by the federal government in 1999, which involves a steady-state payroll tax rate of 9.9 percent. The primary intent of the plan was to accumulate a larger CPP reserve fund to partially "pre-fund" future benefits—it has no impact on LCBRs of the retired or near retired. The main impact of these reforms is to increase the LCBRs of those workers aged 16 to 50 by roughly 0.2, thereby decreasing the LCBRs of the youngest in the population from 2.6 to 2.1 (they will only pay double for what they will receive instead of two and half times). This reform does less for Albertans since the majority of them are in the age groups that take the "hit," and there are relatively fewer older Albertans "spared" from the changes.

Although we have argued that it is inappropriate to view the net CPP outflows from Alberta as a subsidy to the rest of the country, this does not mean that demographic considerations are irrelevant to the province's choice of whom it may choose to pool with for pension purposes. Under the current system, Albertans are pooled with the rest of the country for CPP purposes. One way of viewing an APP is that Albertans would simply be pooling with a different population that has different characteristics. If Alberta maintained the existing structure of the CPP (partially funded PAYGO), but merely pooled with its own population rather than the rest of the country, what does this suggest for the desirability of a separate APP?

Quantifying Alberta's Benefit from an APP
Alberta's demographic advantage *vis-à-vis* the rest of Canada suggests that either contribution rates (payroll taxes) may be lower or benefit rates higher (or some combination thereof) in a contributory APP than such rates are under the CPP. We come to this conclusion by starting with the premise that an APP would grant the same benefits as the existing CPP (including disability and survivors benefits). We then estimate how much lower APP contribution rates could be than CPP contribution rates. To that end, we compare an APP and CPP set up on PAYGO basis with a two-year fund, as per the pre-1999 system. We use the Chief Actuary's pre-reform forecasted payroll tax rates for this scenario. The difference between the CPP and APP contribution rates estimated under this scenario translate easily to the post-1998 system where the increases in the payroll tax rate are accelerated. We assume that the APP and CPP will have the same ratio of

Hypothetical Canada/Alberta Population and CPP/APP Tax Rates, 1996, 2014, 2030

Year	Population of Canada	Population of Alberta	Contribution Rate, Canada (t_C)	Contribution Rate, Alberta (t_A)	Difference (t_C-t_A)
1996	*18–64:* 18,884,263 *65+:* 3,581,991	*18–64:* 1,763,143 *65+:* 271,254	5.6%	4.54%	1.06%
2014	*18–64:* 20,627,280 *65+:* 7,552,931	*18–64:* 2,053,035 *65+:* 615,239	9.7%	7.94%	1.76%
2030	*18–64:* 18,502,153 *65+:* 12,956,123	*18–64:* 1,863,474 *65+:* 1,197,615	14.2%	12.98%	1.22%

benefits to average wages of contributors. We also assume that contributing Albertans pay a tax rate that generates enough revenue to pay the total claims of the retired Albertans. An important point is that we assume that Alberta's share of the two year CPP fund is transferred to the province. Based upon published data on the allocation of interest income generated by the CPP fund among the provinces, Alberta would be entitled to approximately 13 percent of the fund (recall Alberta's higher labour force participation rate). Under these conditions for the APP and CPP, the balanced budget requirements of both plans generates the following relationship between the CPP PAYGO rate and an APP PAYGO rate[5]:

$$t_A = \left(\frac{E_C}{E_A}\right) \cdot \left(\frac{R_A}{R_C}\right) \cdot t_C$$

E_C is the total population of Canadians aged 18 to 64. R_C is the number of people in Canada receiving benefits (total population over age 64 is used in the calculation). t_C is the PAYGO tax rate for Canada. E_A, R_A, and t_A refer to Alberta.

Table 2 presents the hypothetical APP tax rates (t_A) in 1996, 2014, and 2030 compared to the Chief Actuaries forecasted rates for the CPP (t_C). Under this scenario Alberta's demographics dictate that an APP could have a contribution rate that is indeed lower than the CPP rate. In 1996 the difference would have been about 1 percentage point, increasing to 1.76 percentage points by 2014 and falling to 1.22 points by 2030. Although over the next thirty years an APP would face the same demographic pressures as the CPP, thus necessitating an increase in the contribution rates, the level of the contribution rate could be maintained below the CPP rate. With a peak contribution of rate of about 13 percent in 2030, compared to 14.2 percent under the CPP, an APP would lessen but not negate the demographic impact of an aging population.

As indicated above, the recent CPP reforms involve an accelerated increase in the CPP rate to 9.9 percent in 2003, and a concomitant increase in the fund from two to five years. The investment returns generated by this larger fund (assumed by the Actuary to be 3.8 percent per year in real terms), will allow the payroll tax rate to be lower than the 14.2 percent rate projected for 2030. If the APP followed a similar strategy, it too would be able to accelerate the APP payroll tax rate and build up a similar fund. The calculations above suggest that this steady-state rate could be in the neighbourhood of 1.75 percentage points lower than the CPP rate (8.15 percent rather than 9.9 percent). For individuals paying the maximum rate, this generates savings of about $578 per year[6].

While our calculations show that demographics alone allow for a lower APP contribution rate, several other factors may act to mitigate this advantage. First, Albertans will have to pay for the administration of the APP. Alberta currently does not collect payroll taxes of any kind and would incur sizeable set-up costs to establish the appropriate infrastructure to collect such taxes and distribute benefits. (Unlike some other provinces, Alberta Health levies are imposed upon individuals and not collected through payroll taxes.) One possible exception to this is the existing Worker's Compensation Program; it is conceivable that some economies of scale could be realized by rolling APP administration in with the Worker's Compensation Board. However, worker's compensation does not cover all employers or employees, nor, obviously, most retired individuals. In any case, the possibility of economies of scale in tax collection and benefit distribution suggests that Alberta's administration costs may be proportionately greater than the CPP. Although it is difficult to estimate how much larger the extra administration costs in Alberta would be, we do know these costs were one reason Ontario decided not to set up a separate provincial plan in the 1960s.

The second mitigating factor comes from our point that an APP similar in structure to the CPP can be viewed simply as pooling over a different population. Although the APP population would be younger, it would also be smaller and less diverse, which means that it would be riskier. In particular, an APP would be more vulnerable to economic, demographic, and migration shocks—shocks that tend to average out over all of Canada in the CPP. This is particularly important in a resource-based economy such as Alberta, where aggregate earnings, employment, labour force participation, and migration tend to ebb and flow with commodity prices. Indeed, in another context, McKenzie and Kneebone (1999) argue that, all else being equal, sustainable fiscal policy requires that economies with more volatile tax bases have higher average tax rates. In terms of the variability of real GDP growth, Alberta has one of the most volatile economies in the country (McKenzie and Kneebone 1997). This suggests a higher required APP contribution rate due to Alberta's riskier population and economy.

Another potentially important factor involves the fiscally induced migration that may be expected to take place in response to an APP that pays the same benefits with lower contribution rates. If labour is relatively mobile and all else is equal, this additional "Alberta Advantage" may result in a migration of workers to Alberta, which could depress wage growth. This would act just like an increase in the payroll tax rate, thus increasing the "effective" APP contribution rate. Although it is difficult to determine the magnitude of this type of fiscally induced migration, there is some evidence that it does exist. Fiscally induced migration is a common reason given against decentralization of social programs. This cost of decentralization must be traded-off against possible benefits, including the benefits of policy experimentation and competition.

Although we are unable to quantify the above mitigating effects, given the relatively small reduction (at most 1.75 percentage points) in the APP versus CPP contribution rate we calculate, we find it reasonable to conclude that an APP advantage over the CPP for Albertans would be minimal. In fact, once other considerations are factored in (such as the cost of setting up and administering a separate APP, the added risk of pooling with a smaller population, and the impact of Alberta's economic volatility on the level of contribution rates), it is possible that an APP would be more costly for Albertans than remaining in the CPP.

◼️ A FULLY FUNDED APP?

In the preceding section we have argued that the benefits of an APP that mimics the basic structure of the CPP could be quite small. The possibility still remains that Albertans would choose an APP because it would give them the opportunity to have a "fully funded" defined contribution plan in Alberta as opposed to a defined benefit plan such as the CPP. Ignoring the questions of whether or not Albertans would want to make this change, what the investment rules would be, and whether or not such change would be permissible under existing constitutional arrangements, a fully funded APP raises two major issues. The first concerns the costs of making the transition from the CPP to a fully funded APP, the second concerns the portability of APP benefits under this arrangement. We focus on some key points; Robert Brown discusses some of these issues in more detail in the next chapter.

The Cost of Transition from the CPP to a Fully Funded APP

Perhaps the most important detail concerning the transition from the CPP to an APP is the status of CPP benefits currently paid to retired Albertans and the CPP benefit entitlements of working Albertans. We will first consider the retired and then the working Albertans with CPP entitlements. Given that the CPP is effectively funded on a PAYGO basis, current CPP revenues are used to pay current CPP benefits. If Alberta exits the CPP to set up a fully funded APP, who will pay the CPP benefits of retired Albertans? In the PAYGO scenario analyzed in the previous section, we presumed that Alberta would leave with a share of the CPP fund and be responsible for the existing CPP entitlements of Albertans. Things are not so simple in the case of a fully funded APP.

One option is that no new CPP entitlements would accrue to Albertans after transition, but existing entitlements would be honoured by the CPP. In other words, after the transition, CPP revenues would pay out the accumulated CPP entitlements. Given that one reason for Alberta wanting an APP is its age composition and that the province has proportionately more contributors than recipients, the rest of Canada would have to face even higher payroll taxes than currently scheduled. Thus, an APP entails a negative demographic "shock" to the CPP, since it loses more contributors than recipients. For this reason the rest of Canada has an incentive to try to stop Alberta from setting up an APP or to forfeit CPP entitlements of Albertans as a condition of separation.

Given the relatively small proportion of Alberta's population that is retired and collecting CPP benefits, Albertans may be comfortable assuming full responsibility for paying equivalent benefits to retired Albertans. At least in the short run this would result in a lower contribution rate for Albertans in an APP than they would have in the CPP, since a lower proportion of the population in Alberta is retired than the proportion in all of Canada.

The more troubling problem with a transition to a separate fully funded plan concerns the CPP benefit entitlements earned prior to transition by Albertans who are still working. At either the national or provincial level, a switch from a PAYGO plan to a fully funded plan turns the implicit unfunded liability of the PAYGO plan into an explicit liability in the form of entitlement debt. As Jim Pesando (1997, 11) points out in his analysis of a privatized fully funded plan for the entire country:

> Older members of the transition generation will have accrued pension credits under the CPP based on contributions that, if augmented

by a market rate of interest, are not sufficient to pay for the benefits to which the system entitles them.

The government (federal or provincial) has two options to solve this problem. One is not to honour the CPP entitlements at all and impose substantial costs on older workers. This is unlikely to be politically feasible. Therefore the government would have to find some other mechanism to honour CPP obligations over the transition. Pesando advocates offering "recognition bonds" to workers with CPP entitlements. The bonds would represent the present value of the future entitlements and would pay a market interest rate until they become due at retirement. The government would have to use general tax revenues to retire the bonds or levy a payroll tax explicitly to raise this revenue. If the revenue came from general revenues, the government would likely have to increase debt, cut spending, increase other tax rates (such as the personal income tax), or introduce an entirely new tax. In other words, financing the existing CPP obligations would involve explicit costs over and above the contributions required to fully fund benefits comparable to the CPP.

What would these costs be? First we must recognize the "base" costs of a fully funded CPP—the rate a Canadian contributing starting at age 18 would pay to finance only his/her own retirement benefits. Pesando (1997) reports that the full-funding contribution rate for a contributory plan that paid benefits comparable to the CPP is 7 percent. (This is based upon a real rate of return of 3.8 percent per annum.) This full-funding contribution rate is only 2.9 percentage points lower than the steady-state CPP rate and only 1.15 percentage points lower than our calculated steady-state PAYGO APP rate under partial funding

Now we must add the extra costs necessary to retire the unfunded liability, that is, the accrued CPP liabilities at the date of transition. To finance the existing debt, workers would have to pay an additional 2.9 percent. When added to the 7 percent necessary to operate a full-funded plan, the total contribution rate rises to 9.9 percent. A contribution rate of 9.9 percent with a benefit rate of only 7 percent gives an LCBR of 1.4. This is similar to what the average Canadian faced prior to the 1997 CPP reforms. In other words, full funding of the CPP does nothing for the average Canadian. Although full funding clearly benefits younger Canadians (those under age 30) who faced LCBRs under the pre-1997 CPP PAYGO arrangement of as high as 2.6, this benefit comes at a cost to older workers. Moving to full funding from PAYGO benefits the 41 percent of the Canadian population under age 30 in 1996, but harms the 46 percent of Canadians aged 30 to 64 in 1996. Once Canadians recognize the impact of the CPP entitlements, full funding may not be politically saleable in Canada or Alberta.

Separation to a fully funded APP, however, presents a problem even more complex than a change to a fully funded plan on a national level. First, with the creation of an APP, who would issue it "recognition" or "entitlement" bonds for the pension wealth of Albertans? The rest of Canada may not feel obligated to honour CPP entitlements if Albertans voluntarily abandon the CPP. Since Alberta's exit from the CPP would impose a cost on the rest of Canada, Alberta would likely be expected to bear some, if not most, of the transition burden. In the next chapter Robert Brown calculates that Alberta's share of the CPP entitlement liability is about $50 billion. At a 5 percent interest rate this requires $2.5 billion *per year* just to carry this liability, much less retire it. This in and of itself would seem to be enough to swamp any benefits from a fully funded APP for some time to come.

Furthermore, with Alberta's volatile economy and an APP's potentially higher administration costs, it is possible that the contribution rate required to secure comparable benefits to the partially funded CPP will be higher than 9.9 percent. The LCBR for a contribution rate of 11 percent is 1.57; for 12 percent, 1.71; and for 14 percent, 2.0. It does not take a large increase in "administration costs" or "transaction costs" before full funding is a poorer paying proposition for most Albertans over age 25 than even the pure PAYGO CPP was before 1997.

Portability

An APP that mimics the CPP maintains the portability of public pensions in Canada, much like the co-existence of the QPP does today. With a substantially different APP, the question of portability becomes important. Portability of benefits would appear to be more complicated and costly in a funded APP unless the rest of the country goes along. A privatized, individualized, defined contribution approach may be the best way to go in this regard, as retirement accounts could simply follow individuals as they change residences (as is the case with RRSPs). Canadians who change provinces could be treated just like individuals who enter and leave the country. Migrants into Alberta would be entitled to the CPP benefits they earned outside of Alberta, and would begin paying into their APP retirement account upon entry. Migrants out of Alberta would take their APP pension accounts with them, and would begin paying into and earning CPP entitlements. Nonetheless, it seems clear that this would entail higher administrative costs than the current system. To the extent that pension benefits are not portable, there is a danger that labour mobility will be reduced due to "pension lock-in."

The Macroeconomic Impacts of Fully Funded Pension Plans

Finally, although it is not our intention to directly enter the debate regarding the benefits of PAYGO versus fully funded public pensions, one aspect of that debate does deserve mention. One of the benefits of a fully funded approach to contributory public pensions often mentioned is the macroeconomic impact. It is argued (see Feldstein (1976 and 1982) and Leimer and Lesnoy (1982)) that one possible problem with a PAYGO scheme is that it may lower the amount of savings in the economy.

There is some debate on this issue because PAYGO programs have two offsetting impacts on saving. The first impact, the so-called "asset substitution effect," suggests that private saving will fall with the introduction of a PAYGO scheme because individuals no longer need to save as much for retirement. Because the plan is PAYGO, with contributions immediately paid out as benefits, there is also no offsetting increase in government saving. Opposed to the asset substitution effect is the so-called "induced retirement effect." It argues that under a PAYGO system, individuals have an incentive to retire early to realize the pension benefits and this induced early retirement may well cause them to save more. There is some controversy in the empirical literature as to which effect dominates.

Why is this relevant to our discussion? If the asset substitution effect dominates, as Feldstein argues it does, then saving will go up with the movement to a fully funded system. In a closed economy this will lower interest rates, promoting investment and growth. If Feldstein is right, then an APP could increase the savings of Albertans covered under the plan. The problem is that Alberta is a small open economy. Indeed, Canada as a whole is a small open economy, so Alberta is a small open economy within a small open economy. This means that Albertans effectively treat the interest rate as given, and increased savings in Alberta will have no impact on the interest rate. Thus, a fully funded separate APP would not generate more investment or economic growth in Alberta, would not have a macroeconomic impact, and would lack one of the more important benefits of a fully funded pension[7].

■■■ CONCLUSIONS

Alberta's demographics suggest that the PAYGO contribution rates under a separate APP may be lower than the CPP, at least in the short run. We estimate that the APP payroll tax rate under PAYGO could be at most 1.75 percentage points lower than the comparable CPP rate. However, the volatility of Alberta's economy, increased administration costs, increased risk from pooling within a smaller population, and the effects of fiscally induced migration could easily erode this rate reduction, rendering it insignificant.

Under a fully funded APP scenario, the issue of existing CPP entitlements of working and retired Albertans must be resolved. With the obligations of accumulated CPP entitlements, Alberta's contribution rate would have to incorporate the costs of servicing and retiring this explicit CPP debt over the short and the long term. Whether forming a separate APP or remaining in the CPP is better for Albertans depends on whether the contribution rate relief afforded by demographics in the short run or the benefits of a fundamentally redesigned pension scheme more than compensate for the increased tax burdens associated with the explicit CPP debt issued at the date of transition. Our crude estimates show that full-funding does nothing to help Canadians over age 30 in 1996, when compared to the PAYGO CPP. If scale economies exist in the administration of pension plans, we should also include the increased per capita costs of administering the smaller APP relative to the CPP.

The problem of accumulated CPP entitlements is the primary reason that the Québec Pension Plan (QPP), separate but "harmonized" with the CPP, is not directly a useful model for other provinces in Canada. The QPP was established at the outset of contributory government pension plans in 1966. Essentially, Québec set up its provincial plan with the luxury of no transition costs. Once a province participates in the CPP, exit from the plan becomes increasingly costly to the point that the CPP is a bit like the Eagles' song, "Hotel California": you can check out anytime you like, but you can never really leave. We think that any solution to address the demographic challenges for pensions in Canada should be sought at the federal level; pensions are not a good area for provinces to take over. Finally, for those readers who are just frustrated with CPP reforms in the face of the demographically driven CPP crisis, we offer another line from "Hotel California": *They stab it with their steely knives, but they just can't kill the beast*[8].

Notes

1. Ontario's participation in the plan was vital for Ottawa. As Bryden (1974, 174) points out, "even if Ontario accepted the federal-Québec terms in full, separate administration by that province, with its relatively large number of high income earners, could vitiate the calculations on which some of the benefits in the federal plan were based."

2. The contributions include Alberta's share of the investment income generated by the CPP fund. The benefits include Alberta's share of CPP expenditures on goods and services, which reflect administration expenses; this accounts for a very small amount relative to total expenditures.

3. As an aside, it is interesting to juxtapose these ratios with the fact that Saskatchewan and British Columbia were the only two anglophone provinces not to sign on to the 1997 CPP reforms. As discussed below, the 1997 reforms hit current younger generations relatively hard, with older and currently retired individuals bearing very little of the cost. In light of these considerations it is curious indeed that Alberta, with a younger population, agreed to the reforms while Saskatchewan and British Columbia did not.
4. Complete details of these calculations are given in the appendix following this chapter.
5. Complete details of these calculations are given in the appendix following this chapter.
6. Note that this is the reduction in combined employer and employee contributions.
7. We would like to thank Mel MacMillan for emphasizing this point.
8. Our thanks go to Bev Dahlby for this comparison.

References

Bryden, Kenneth. 1974. *Old Age Pensions and Policy-Making in Canada*. McGill-Queen's University Press.

Feldstein, Martin S. 1976. "Social Security, Induced Retirement, and Aggregate Capital Accumulation." *Journal of Political Economy* 82(5), 77–104.

Feldstein, Martin S. 1982. "Social Security and Private Saving." *Journal of Political Economy* 90(3), 630–642.

Kneebone, Ronald D. and Kenneth J. McKenzie. 1998a. "The Characteristics of Fiscal Policy in Canada." Mimeograph.

Kneebone, Ronald D. and Kenneth J. McKenzie. 1998b. "The Stabilizing Features of Fiscal Policy in Canada." In *Fiscal Targets and Economic Growth*, T. Courchene and T. Wilson eds. Roundtable Series 12. Kingston: The John Deutsch Institute for the Study of Economic Policy and the Institute for Policy Analysis.

Leimer, Dean R. and Selig D. Lesnoy. 1982. "Social Security and Private Savings, New Time-Series Evidence." *Journal of Political Economy* 90(3), 606–629.

Oreopolous, Philip. 1996. "Bad Tasting Medicine: Removing Intergenerational Inequity from the CPP." *Choices* 2(7).

Pesando, James E. 1997. "From Tax Grab to Retirement Saving: Privatizing the CPP Premium Hike." C.D. Howe Institute Commentary 93. Toronto: C.D. Howe Institute.

Statistics Canada. CANSIM Matrices 2064 (Canada, Basic Labour Force Characteristics), 2094 (Alberta, Basic Labour Force Characteristics), 6367 (Population by Single Years of Age, Age Groups and Sex, For Canada, Provinces and Territories, July 1), 6376 (Population by Single Years of Age, Age Groups and Sex, For Alberta, July 1).

Alberta Report, 17 November, 1997
Globe and Mail, 6 November 1997, A27

Appendix 1: Data and Data Sources

Average Lifetime Contribution-Benefit Ratios for Alberta and Canada

The Lifetime Contribution Benefit Ratios (LCBRs) by single years of age have been "eyeballed" from Oreopolous (1996). Two of Oreopolous' scenarios were used. First, the pure PAYGO approach that would have seen contribution rates rise to 14.2 by 2030. Second, the partially funded approach that accelerates the rate of increase in contribution rates to 10.8 percent within 7 years where it remains forever. This latter case overstates the level of the "steady-state" contribution of rate 9.9 percent which the Liberal government committed to in 1997, but otherwise closely approximates the changes to the CPP in 1997. The age-specific LCBRs are then weighted by the appropriate percentages of population in both Canada and Alberta to determine an average LCBR.

Table 2: Hypothetical APP Contribution Rates

These numbers were calculated for a PAYGO basis of financing the APP. They are based upon the PAYGO rates that were forecast for the CPP in 1996. Other assumptions held are that administration costs for the APP and CPP are zero and that the ratio of the annual benefit to average wages is the same for Alberta and Canada. Population numbers are from CANSIM Matrices 6367 and 6376. For 1996, the size of the retired populations is the actual numbers of individuals aged 65 and over. For 2014, the population aged 0 to 46 in 1996 is the population aged 18 to 64. The retired population in 2014 is the population aged 47 to 74 in 1996. These population forecasts assume no mortality or migration. Every one dies after age 92 by assumption. For 2030 the same exercise is carried out. To account for the aging of 15 years of unborn Albertans and Canadians, we assume that average number of Albertans and Canadians under age 15 in 1996 is the number for each of the 15 years of unborn Albertans and Canadians. That is, for ages "-1" to "-15" in 1996, we assume there are 39,000 Albertans and 390,000 Canadians in each year.

The hypothetical contribution rates are calculated based on the following derivation based upon the budget constraints for PAYGO plans:

$$w_j \cdot E_j \cdot t_j - B_j \cdot R_j = 0 \quad j = A, C$$

$$t_j \cdot \frac{E_j}{R_j} - \frac{B_j}{w_j} = 0$$

$$t_A \cdot \frac{E_A}{R_A} - \frac{B_A}{w_A} = 0 = t_C \cdot \frac{E_C}{R_C} - \frac{B_C}{w_C}$$

$$\text{if } \frac{B_A}{w_A} = \frac{R_A}{w_C} \text{ then}$$

$$t_A = \left(\frac{E_C}{E_A}\right) \cdot \left(\frac{R_A}{R_C}\right) \cdot t_C$$

A refers to Alberta, *C* to Canada. w_j is the average amount of earnings of the people in population *j*. E_j is the number of people in population *j* between ages 18 and 64 (total population aged 18 to 64 is used in the calculation). R_j is the number of people in population *j* receiving benefits (total population over age 64 in jurisdiction *j* is used in the calculation). B_j is the average amount of benefits paid to recipients in population *j*. t_C is the PAYGO tax rate for Canada. The Chief Actuary's forecast of CPP PAYGO contribution rates is used.

ROBERT L. BROWN

Alberta Opting Out of the Canada Pension Plan

Can It Be Done?
Should It Be Done?

THIS CHAPTER IS WRITTEN in two distinct parts. The first section outlines the process that would have to be followed if Alberta decided that it wished to opt out of the Canada Pension Plan (CPP). In the second part of the chapter, I analyze the advantages and disadvantages of the current CPP system and its most logical alternative, fully funded Mandatory Retirement Savings Plans. Because I find this alternative deficient for a variety of reasons, I conclude that Albertans should stay in the CPP and work to keep it as a viable social security scheme.

▬▬ OPTING OUT OF THE CANADA PENSION PLAN: THE PROCESS

What is required for any province to opt out of the CPP? What are the implications if Alberta were to attempt to do so? First there are several legal aspects. The CPP Act is a federal act applying to all provinces on a mandatory basis. However, any province is free to set up its own contributory earnings-related pension plan provided the provincial plan is similar to the CPP. The CPP Act does not specify what "similar" means exactly, but it is generally understood that both the benefit provisions (retirement, disability, and survivor) and the financing approach of any new plan would have to be highly similar to the CPP (for example, the provincial plan would need to have similar contribution rates).

One successful example of opting out is the Québec decision to form the Québec Pension Plan (QPP), which runs in parallel to the CPP. It must be noted, however, that the QPP is fundamentally similar to the CPP, to the extent that the contribution rate is the same and workers can move from Québec to other provinces (and vice versa) without having to worry about any potential impact on their social security benefits. Québec has made some modifications to the QPP (such as the 1984 move to permit a flexible retirement age) that might be argued to have made the plans measurably different. However, Québec was able to do so without formal approval (in this example, the CPP was amended to allow flexible retirement ages in 1987).

Any modification to the CPP having a material impact on the plan can be implemented only if at least two-thirds of the provinces covering at least two-thirds of the Canadian population consent to it. The vote to allow modifications to the CPP includes Québec, despite the fact that it runs its own parallel plan. This effectively gives Ontario a veto on any material change to the CPP; Québec, with minor support from other provinces, has the same power to stop change.

Any province wishing to opt out of the CPP in a manner that would not have material effect on the cost of the CPP can do so freely (without being subject to the formal consent process). However, it would have to set up simultaneously a plan very similar to the CPP for its working population (such as the QPP). The main implication of setting up a similar provincial plan is that the province chooses to become responsible for the administration of the plan (collection of contributions, payment of benefits, investment of the account, and so on). A province wishing to opt out of the CPP to set up a materially different plan (such as mandatory RRSPs) would have to go through the formal consent process.

Alberta also faces financial implications if it chooses to opt out of the CPP. It would likely want to claim its share of the CPP account (the so-called CPP assets). At this time, all CPP assets are invested in provincial government bonds in proportion to the contributions from the province. Thus, Alberta would be claiming back about $4 billion in Alberta bonds. These can hardly be viewed as true assets to the province.

If Alberta gets approval to opt out, the province then also becomes responsible for the actuarial liability within the CPP of the benefits that its workers have accrued to date. The Alberta share of the CPP accrued liabilities would be almost exactly $50 billion—$46 billion unfunded, and $4 billion backed by Alberta bonds (personal communication with the Office of the Superintendent of Financial Institutions [OSFI]).

The province has at least the following two choices regarding the payment of these "accrued" benefits:

1. pay an administrative fee to the CPP for paying of accrued benefits by the CPP administration in Ottawa which has all the records on file (that is, pay Ottawa $46 billion);
2. take immediate responsibility for administering the payment of all benefits (those $50 billion worth of benefits accrued to date, plus all future benefits) and pay Ottawa a small fee for the transfer of administrative records and data from the CPP files.

Clearly, then, on the first morning of independent operation Alberta will be faced with the task of determining how to finance the $50 billion in accrued benefit promises. Within the CPP, this would be funded by future contributions and investment income. This could also be done in Alberta through earmarked contributions or taxes. However, if Alberta is also going to establish a fully funded scheme for all new benefit accruals, then the present working generation will have to pay two bills coincidentally. First, they will have to pay the $50 billion in accrued benefits under the old scheme, and, second, they will also have to pre-fund their own future benefits. That may prove to be a difficult sell.

As a result of Alberta's opting out, the CPP might have to be revised actuarially. Alberta has a young and above-average-income population. Thus, the opting out of Alberta would likely have a small but measurable negative impact on the remaining plan. In short, I expect the CPP pay-as-you-go (PAYGO) contribution rate to be slightly higher without Alberta than with it.

To summarize, Alberta can "opt out" of the CPP with little difficulty if it wishes to establish an almost-identical plan for its residents. That would make little sense, however, as the administrative costs of the two plans would have to be higher than they are today in a consolidated plan. To opt out and establish a dissimilar plan, as I anticipate, Alberta would need the approval of two-thirds of the provinces with two-thirds of the population (this includes Québec).

Opting out at this time might be easier than at some future date. First, it is doubtful that the present government in Ontario would oppose such an "experiment" by Alberta. Rather, I would expect Ontario to support this partial privatization of the CPP with Alberta leading the way. (Remember that the support of Ontario is essential given the approval formula.) I would expect to find opposition from "left-leaning" governments, which at this time include British Columbia, Saskatchewan, and Québec. However, Québec might support Alberta's move purely to create dissonance in the rest of Canada.

A second reason for attempting this move at this time is the lack of complication in dividing up the CPP assets. To date, all CPP cashflow surpluses have been lent to the provinces in proportion to their contributions. Thus, it is clear that the Alberta share of the CPP assets is simply the Alberta bonds within the asset pool. No problem. However, Paul Martin has announced a dramatic hike in contribution rates, from 6 percent to 9.9 percent over five years, which will create significant cashflow surpluses. These surpluses are to be invested in the private sector by an independent investment advisory board. Thus, if Alberta were to wait several years, it might be far less clear just which assets (such as large real estate holdings) belong to Alberta and which do not.

Thus, if there is a good time to break up the CPP, perhaps it is now. More important, however, should the CPP be broken up?

■■■■ ADVANTAGES OF THE PRESENT CPP STRUCTURE

Although the CPP and, in particular its previous method of PAYGO financing, have been highly criticized, to date the CPP has been an overwhelming success story. Primarily because of its existence, poverty rates among the elderly have plummeted. Between 1971 and 1985, the proportion of the elderly receiving CPP/QPP benefits increased from less than 15 percent to almost 60 percent (Dickinson 1994, A-I-18). Poverty, measured using the Statistics Canada "low-income" criteria for the elderly, fell from 33.6 percent in 1980 to 16.9 percent in 1995 (National Council 1997, 13). For couples 65 and older, the poverty rate has fallen from 22.2 percent in 1980 to 7.5 percent in 1995 (National Council 1997, 17). Many of these poverty rates are record or near-record lows (National Council 1997, 87). Ivan Fellegi (1988, 4.8) considers the maturing of the CPP and QPP to be the most important factor contributing to this drop in the poverty rate among the elderly[1]. Thus, the CPP has met and even surpassed the benefit promises made at its inception (CPP benefits have increased significantly over the years).

The PAYGO financing basis of the CPP has also been highly criticized. PAYGO financing (where today's benefits are paid out of today's contributions, with no surplus accruing) is highly dependent on the ratio of retirees to workers. In fact, the contribution rate required for any PAYGO system is a direct function of total national income (Treuil 1981). National income, in turn, is a function of the size of the population of working age, the labour force participation rate, and productivity of the workers. (Thus, increasing the labour force participation rate of females, or increasing net immigration of qualified workers, or increasing worker productivity is as helpful to the financing requirements of a PAYGO system as an increase in the birth rate.)

While PAYGO financing has the disadvantage of being demographically sensitive, there are several advantages of government-sponsored PAYGO schemes:

1. The entire working population can be covered relatively easily. Presently, only 47 percent of workers are covered by employer pension plans (this includes only 33 percent of private sector workers) (Statistics Canada 1997).
2. Benefits can be immediately vested and are fully portable, important features for today's mobile work force (features that are not achieved by private plans).

| Year | Life Expectancy (years) | | | | | |
| | At Birth | | At Age 65 | | At Age 75 | |
	Male	Female	Male	Female	Male	Female
1921	58.8	60.6	13.0	13.6	7.6	8.0
1941	63.0	66.3	12.8	14.1	7.5	8.2
1961	68.4	74.2	13.5	16.1	8.2	9.5
1981	71.9	79.0	14.6	18.9	9.0	11.9
1991	74.6	80.9	15.7	19.9	9.6	12.5

Source: *Statistics Canada (Nagnur, Dhruva 1986)*
Life Tables, Canada and the Provinces, 1985–1987
Life Tables, Canada and the Provinces, 1990–1992 (Statistics Canada, 1995)

3. Because contribution income immediately becomes benefit payout, no problem exists with indexing benefits to wages. In fact, there exists a source of "actuarial discounting" for years with real productivity gains if benefits are indexed to cost of living and contributions are indexed to average wages (the norm). Indexation has remained only a future hope for private plans.

4. Administrative costs are usually very low per unit of cashflow, much lower than for private plans. The CPP administrative costs are only 1.3 percent of cashflow (OSFI 1998). For the QPP, administration costs are also 1.3 percent (Québec 1995), plus a charge of 0.09 percent against the investment return for direct investment expenses of the Caisse de dépôts et placements du Québec (CDPQ). No private plan operates at expense ratios that are this low. Many smaller private plans have expense ratios four to five times as large, thus negating any extra gross rate of return on assets of a pre-funded plan. (An Alberta Pension Plan could not expect to have an expense ratio as low as the CPP because of its much smaller size.)

▬▬▶ WHY THE INTEREST IN FULLY FUNDED SCHEMES?

The shift in the ratio of retirees to workers that will occur between now and 2030 is the chief concern around the future viability of all PAYGO schemes. Since Canada is facing a rapidly aging population (defined here as the percentage of the population aged 65 and over), many commentators have referred to the CPP as "bankrupt." There are two causes of this population

Assumption	1960s	Current
Senior Dependency Ratio	0.33	0.40
Annual Increase in Real Wages	2.0%	1.0%
Real Interest Rates	2.0%	4.0%
Projected Cost (as a Percentage of Payroll):		
PAYGO System	11.0%	14.5%
Fully Funded System	16.5%	7.2%

Source: *Canadian Institute of Actuaries (1994, 22–23).*

aging. The first cause is a significant improvement in life expectancy, especially for females (see Table 1). More importantly, Canada has experienced significant drops in the number of live births in the period since its peak in 1959, and especially since the end of the baby-boom in 1966. This has become known as the baby-boom/baby-bust cycle (see Foot and Stoffman, 1996).

In the early 1960s, when the CPP and QPP were designed, demographic and economic variables favoured PAYGO financing. In particular, as stated in the Canadian Institute of Actuaries (CIA) paper *Troubled Tomorrows* (1994, 22–23), long-term financing assumptions at that time would have estimated the projected costs (as a percentage of payroll) for a PAYGO system to be 11.0 percent, compared to 16.5 percent for a fully funded system (see Table 2). But times have changed. The future isn't what it used to be. Today's long-term assumptions shift the balance to 14.5 percent of payroll for a PAYGO system and 7.2 percent for a fully funded one (Table 2). Thus the following statement from Keith Ambachtsheer seems logical (1995):

> Just as pay-go financing makes sense when real interest rates are lower than real GDP growth prospects (i.e., the mid-1960s), so a conversion to pre-funding makes sense when real interest rates are higher than real GDP growth prospects (i.e., the mid-1990s).

The problem with this conclusion is that the requisite relationships are unsustainable. The debt must be reduced; inflation must continue to be controlled. Those who argue for privatization of social security agree that those goals are necessities. But the result of a lower debt ratio and controlled inflation should be lower interest rates and higher GDP growth, the financing assumptions that would once again favour a PAYGO arrangement. As the CIA report (1995, 23) wisely concludes:

> Should Canada abandon the pay-as-you-go approach? We think not. No retirement income system—funded or unfunded, public or private—is free from risk. Any attempt to fund or replace Canada's public pension plans will be expensive in the short term, with no guarantee of a commensurate reduction in long-term cost. Today's environment favours funded retirement savings plans, but tomorrow's environment, like the environment of the 1960s, might not.

⬤▬▬ EVALUATING THE ALTERNATIVE— A FULLY FUNDED PLAN

Is a Fully Funded Pension Demographically Immune?

Clearly the most serious problem facing PAYGO social security is the rapidly shifting ratio of retirees to workers over the next 40 years. Would a fully funded social security system (such as Mandatory Retirement Savings Plans) be demographically immune?

One of the problems that exists with any discussion around the optimal financing arrangement for social security is confusion between what is true on a microeconomic basis (for one person or a small group) and what is true on a macroeconomic basis. The assumption that what is true for an individual will necessarily be true in aggregate is sometimes referred to as the *Fallacy of Composition*. To illustrate: if I stand up at a concert, I can see better, but if everyone stands, then no one has an improved view.

Clearly, for an individual to save for retirement, that individual must forgo consumption during his/her working lifetime and set money aside in savings. These funds will then used to buy goods and services post-retirement. This system appears to be workable regardless of the ratio of retirees to workers since every worker funds his/her own benefits in full. Thus, it would seem logical for a nation to provide for its citizens' post-retirement needs by designing a fully funded social security scheme that accumulates enough money to buy everyone's full post-retirement consumption needs.

Francisco Bayo, Chief Actuary of OASDI, says this will, in fact, not work:

> For Social Security, you cannot accumulate assets; that is, claims from somebody else's production. If we have a large amount of money in the Social Security trust funds, we have a claim on ourselves, which does not have much meaning. The truth is, whatever is going to be consumed—be it a product that you can get a physical hold of, or services that are very difficult to hold—those products cannot be stockpiled. They have

to be provided at the time of consumption. No matter what kind of financing we are going to have in our Social Security program, you will find that the benefits that will be obtained by the beneficiary in the year 2050 will have to be produced by the workers in the year 2050, or just a few years earlier (1988, 178).

Nicholas Barr says it even more strongly:

The widely held (but false) view that funded schemes are inherently "safer" than PAYGO is an example of the fallacy of composition. For individuals the economic function of a pension scheme is to transfer consumption over time. But (ruling out the case where current output is stored in holes in people's gardens) this is not possible for society as a whole; the consumption of pensioners as a group is produced by the next generation of workers. From an aggregate viewpoint, the economic function of pension schemes is to divide total production between workers and pensioners, i.e., to reduce the consumption of workers so that sufficient output remains for pensioners. Once this point is understood it becomes clear why PAYGO and funded schemes, which are simply ways of dividing output between workers and pensioners, should not fare very differently in the face of demographic change (1993, 220).

So clearly, fully funded social security systems do not overcome the impact of the impending demographic shifts. The pension income of any decade must come out of the national income of that decade. Thus, prefunded or not, a macroeconomic social security system is as dependent on the future generation of workers as is a PAYGO system.

Critiques of Mandatory Retirement Savings Plans
I have made the assumption that Alberta does not plan to opt out of the CPP and establish a highly similar plan in parallel. There appear to be no advantages to this. Further, the federal and provincial governments have just recently agreed to increase the level of prefunding of the CPP (and create an investment fund expected to exceed $110 billion). Thus, it is also not logical to assume that Alberta wishes to opt out solely to increase the level of prefunding while keeping all other features of the CPP intact. Hence, some remarkable "reforms" to the present CPP model must be assumed.

The only logical model that Alberta could have in mind would be replacing the present "defined-benefit" CPP model with a "defined-contribution" system of Mandatory Retirement Savings Plans (MRSPs). This model has been proposed by the Reform Party of Canada and supported by Andrew

Coyne (then of the *Globe and Mail*), the Fraser Institute, and the C. D. Howe Institute. This proposal has some advantages and some disadvantages.

As to advantages, the scheme would allow for universal coverage of workers, immediate vesting, and full portability. It would also provide billions of dollars of investable funds, although where one would find high-yielding and prudent investments is not specified (especially given Canada's 20 percent offshore investment limit). Many support having MRSPs replace defined-benefit Social Security (see, for example, World Bank (1994) and Robson (1996)); their arguments will not be repeated here.

There are, however, also several disadvantages to defined-contribution MRSPs. First, all of the risks of a defined contribution plan, including the investment risk, the inflation risk, and the mortality risk, would fall on the shoulders of the individual worker instead of being shared across the entire Canadian population. As a result one should expect workers to invest in relatively low risk investments which, in turn, will result in lower long-term rates of return than may be modelled today. This is extremely important since every 1 percent of extra return over the lifetime of a worker results in a pension that is about 24 percent larger (Adams 1967).

Second, the ancillary benefits of the present CPP—including disability income benefits, orphans' benefits, and death benefits—would be lost or have to be replaced in some new scheme. These ancillary benefits are 37 percent of the total CPP package of coverage. The Reform Party suggested that participants should buy private insurance to replace these benefits. The Reform proposal, however, did not present costing for such insurance or provide solutions for those who cannot get private coverage.

Third, administrative expenses for such a scheme can be expected to run at 12 to 15 percent of cashflow (as in Chile) versus the 1.3 percent expense ratio for the CPP. Thus any imagined higher gross rates of investment return would most likely be lost to the higher expense ratios. The impact of these additional expenses can be expected to be regressive, since smaller account balances of poorer workers will experience a larger percentage of expenses than larger account balances.

Fourth, there may well not be enough high quality assets available within Canada to match the investable funds that would now be available. In the inevitable periods of poor investment returns the government may be blamed. At the very least, a switch by the government to a defined contribution system at this time will curse the workers with the inevitability of "buying high" and "selling low." This is because these new investment funds will be entering the market place the same time the 10 million baby-boomers are hitting their maximum savings years, and then the funds will be liquidated the same time as the entire baby-boom generation will also be in a liquidation mode.

Fifth, there is no wealth redistribution in the scheme. A worker who is poor throughout his/her working lifetime is guaranteed poverty in retirement. Similarly, the wealthy worker is guaranteed a wealthy retirement, aided by the significant MRSP tax advantages that would be provided by the scheme.

Sixth, without special legislation, women would retire with lower retirement income than men of identical work and contribution records because of the higher female life expectancy. Women would also lose the child-bearing drop-out provisions of the CPP.

Seventh, the transition generation will have to pay twice: first to fund the new defined-contribution scheme and second to pay for the $50 billion accrued liability of Alberta's share of the CPP. In this regard, it must be remembered that it will be 30 to 40 years before the new defined-contribution scheme can pay out full benefits.

Eighth, if the Chilean experience is any indication, there will probably be a need for some government guarantees of minimum benefits and/or minimum investment performance under the new system. Unless designed skilfully, such minimum guarantees could lead to economic distortions and possible worker selection against the system.

Finally, one might question the justification for MRSPs. Since the CPP has an income redistribution component, a general welfare argument can be used to defend such a system. But is there political justification for a free government to force individual saving without wealth redistribution?

The Chilean Model Reviewed

My examination of MRSPs concludes with a review of the Chilean fully funded model. The new Chilean social security system was decreed in 1981. Rather than a government-run PAYGO scheme, as had previously existed in Chile, the new system requires that employees contribute 10 percent of pay to one of fifteen investment fund agencies (called AFPs). Workers also pay approximately 3.5 percent to cover disability income benefits and survivor benefits (provided by private insurance companies). Employers do not contribute, nor do members of the military or the self-employed. At the time that these 13.5 percent contributions were mandated, workers were granted an 18 percent pay increase (employers incurred this increase but saw their large social security contributions disappear).

The government is responsible for all accrued liabilities of the old PAYGO system, and has issued recognition bonds equal in value to the accrued social security benefits for all previous participants who qualify (workers who only had a very short work history under the old social security system were not given any recognition of their accrued benefits). This generation of workers will, in effect, be paying twice, once to fund their own retirement through the new system (through contributions), and once to pay off the recognition bonds for the accrued liabilities of the old PAYGO system (through general taxation).

The government also limits the extent to which the rate of return provided by one pension fund may fall below that of the average AFP rate of return, and, after annuitization, guarantees annuity payments if the insurance company fails (100 percent of the minimum pension is guaranteed, plus 75 percent of the rest of the benefit up to a specified limit). Finally, the government guarantees a minimum benefit under the new system for those who have at least 20 years of coverage under both the old and new plans. The cost of these guarantees will be financed through general tax revenues, which is equivalent to PAYGO financing.

Eighty-six percent of eligible workers are affiliated with the new system, but only fifty-five percent of the labour force are contributing members. This represents a high level of non-compliance, apparently mostly from poor workers who will receive the minimum benefit regardless. Obviously, the system only includes wage and salaried employees (and not homemakers and the like), and retirement benefits are a direct function of lifetime earnings. That is, there is no redistribution of wealth in the system except for the guaranteed minimum benefit. All risks (including the investment risk, inflation, and mortality) are transferred to the individual worker, except for the minimum guarantees listed above.

Under the new plan about 40 percent of total assets are invested in government bonds, which means that to that extent the new plan is still PAYGO. Almost all assets (99.8 percent) are invested in the Chilean economy. This appeared to be sound policy in the early years of the system as rates of return averaged 13 percent. However, in 1995, the AFPs experienced net losses as the Santiago Bourse performed badly (Orgill 1996). There is now general discussion about diversifying the investment funds outside of Chile.

If the new AFP system can earn an average 7 percent real rate of return over the lifetime of the average worker, that the new system should provide benefits as large as the old PAYGO system (assuming only a small change in life expectancy). While the plan did earn such rates in its early years, it has not recently. In the long run, a 7 percent real rate of return is considered to be very high for a mature economy (such as Canada).

AFP expense ratios for sales commissions, advertising, and general administration are high. Myers (1992) reports that they are 15 percent of the contributions (higher for lower wage earners and lower for higher contributors, since part of the fee is flat rate which make them regressive). Some estimates now put total sales costs as high as 26 percent of contributions (Orgill 1996), as sales people, trying to maximize their commissions, encourage members to switch funds often. This is such a concern that Chile is considering placing restrictions on the ability to switch (such restrictions already exist in Argentina). These Chilean expense ratios compare to ratios of 1.3 percent for the CPP and QPP.

In 1980, under the old PAYGO financing system, gross national savings in Chile were 21.0 percent of GDP. After the introduction of the new mandatory individual savings scheme, savings rates dipped in the 1980s and stood at 18.8 percent of GDP in 1991 (Uthoff 1993).

So while the Chilean system of mandatory individual savings accounts has been studied and touted as a model from Britain to Uzbekistan, Chile's free-market pension system is suddenly facing a host of challenges: falling returns, soaring costs, and an over-dependence on local economic savings (Orgill 1996).

■■■ CONCLUSION

I began this chapter by outlining the process that would have to be followed if Alberta were to decide that it wished to opt out of the Canada Pension Plan (CPP). Opting out seems to be possible, but not without potential difficulties and financial pain. Then I considered the advantages and disadvantages of the current system and the alternatives that Alberta might be considering to replace the CPP benefits for its citizens. In particular, I focussed on MRSPs and concluded that they were deficient for a variety of reasons. In my opinion, therefore, it would be in the best interests of Albertans to stay in the CPP and work to keep it as a viable social security scheme.

Notes

1. The other major factors are substantial increases in the Guaranteed Income Supplement, introduction of the Spouse's Allowance program, and a noticeable increase in private pension income because more people either are being covered by such plans or have Registered Retirement Savings Plans (RRSPs).

References

Adams, W.R. 1967. "The Effect of Interest on Pension Contributions." In *Transactions of the Society of Actuaries*, Vol. XIX. Chicago: University of Chicago Press.

Ambachtsheer, Keith. 1995. *The Ambachtsheer Letter*. #157 Toronto.

Barr, Nicholas. 1993. *The Economics of the Welfare State*. London: Weidenfeld and Nicolson.

Bayo, F. 1988. "Measures of Actuarial Balance for Social Insurance Programs." *Record, the Society of Actuaries*. 14(1), 161–179; ChicVolume 46, 1–32.

Canadian Institute of Actuaries. 1995. *Troubled Tomorrows: The Report of the Canadian Institute of Actuaries' Task Force on Retirement Savings*. Ottawa: Canadian Institute of Actuaries.

Dickinson, P. T. 1994. *A Study for the Evaluation of the Canada Pension Plan's Retirement Pension*. Ottawa: Human Resource Development Canada.

Fellegi, Ivan P. 1988. "Can We Afford an Aging Society?" *Canadian Economic Observer*, October. Ottawa: Statistics Canada.

Foot, David K. with D. Stoffman. 1996. *Boom, Bust, and Echo.* Toronto: Macfarlane, Walter and Ross.

Myers, Robert J. 1992. "Chile's Social Security Reform (After Ten Years)." *Benefits Quarterly* (International Society of Certified Employer Benefit Specialists), 8(3), 41–55.

National Council of Welfare. 1997. *Poverty Profile, 1995* (Ottawa: Minister of Supply and Services, Canada), Autumn.

Office of the Superintendent of Financial Institutions (OSFI). 1998. *Canada Pension Plan: Seventeenth Actuarial Report as at December 31, 1998.* Ottawa.

Robson, W. B. P. 1996. *Putting Some Gold in the Golden Years: Fixing the Canada Pension Plan.* C.D. Howe Institute Commentary 76. Toronto: C.D. Howe Institute.

Statistics Canada (Nagnur, Dhruva). 1986. *Longevity and Historical Life Tables, 1921–1981 (Abridged), Canada and the Provinces, 1986.* Ottawa: Ministry of Supply and Services.

Statistics Canada. 1995. *Life Tables, Canada and the Provinces, 1990–1992.* Catalogue No. 84-537. Ottawa: Ministry of Industry, Science and Technology.

Statistics Canada. 1997. *Pension Plans in Canada, January 1996.* Catalogue No. 74-401. Ottawa: Ministry of Industry.

Treuil, Pierre. 1981. "Fund Development of an Earnings-Related Social Insurance Plan under Stabilized Conditions." In *Transactions of the Society of Actuaries,* Vol. XXXIII. Chicago: University of Chicago Press.

Uthoff, A. W. 1993. "Pension System Reform in Latin America." In *Finance and the Real Economy,* Y. Akyuz, G. Held, ECLAC, UNCTAD, UNU (eds). Santiago, Chile.

World Bank. 1994. *Averting the Old Age Crisis: Policies to Protect the Old and Promote Growth.* A World Bank Policy Research Project. New York: Oxford University Press.

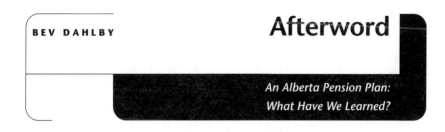

BEV DAHLBY

Afterword

An Alberta Pension Plan: What Have We Learned?

IN THIS CHAPTER, I summarize the prospects for an Alberta Pension Plan (APP) as discussed in the previous four chapters. I will also point out what we don't know and should know if we are to make informed decisions about the future of the public pension system in Alberta and Canada.

⬛ PRECARIOUS PYRAMID: THE ECONOMICS AND POLITICS OF THE CPP

William Robson reviews the nature of the Canada Pension Plan (CPP) and the options for reforming it. He describes the intergenerational transfers that are inherent in a pay-as-you-go (PAYGO) public pension scheme, such as the CPP. Robson reminds us that the 1960s were a period of abnormal economic conditions in which the growth rate of the economy exceeded the real rate of return on financial assets. These conditions made the Ponzi game of PAYGO public pensions appear socially beneficial. It is not surprising that the CPP was designed as a PAYGO pension scheme, with only a relatively small fund to cushion against short-term economic shocks.

In my view, the problem with the CPP is not the PAYGO system but our inability to address the under-funding of the CPP in a timely manner. Although the need to adjust the CPP was evident by the end of the 1970s, no serious attempts were made to address the issue until the late 1990s. Indeed, the changes made to the CPP in the 1970s and 1980s contributed to the under-funding problem. Uncertainty about future demographic trends and economic conditions raises concerns about the viability of the CPP, and we need to be able to adjust the CPP in light of new information about these trends. It has been very difficult to adjust the basic parameters of the CPP because any adjustment requires the agreement of a coalition of provinces and the federal government. An interesting question for future research, and one I hope that Robson pursues, is whether more timely adjustments to a public pension system are likely on a provincial basis rather than on a national basis. In other words, could an APP adjust more quickly to new information on economic and demographic trends than the CPP? Sometimes smaller, more homogeneous political units find it easier to make fiscal adjustments than larger, more heterogeneous units because the larger units have more difficulty in forming the consensus needed to implement policy reforms. For example, the provinces who first presented balanced budgets—Alberta, New Brunswick, and Saskatchewan—were (for the most part) smaller than the provinces that were slow to recognize the need for fiscal adjustment—Ontario, Québec, and British Columbia, as well as the federal government.

Robson also considers the problem of reforming public pension plans. Along with other researchers, he has shown that future generations will receive less from the CPP than they would have from a fully funded pension plan earning a 4.0 percent rate of return on contributions. This growing recognition of the need for reforms explains why the majority of current contributors have been willing to pay the higher contribution rate, scheduled to increase to 9.9 percent by the year 2003. As Robson ably points out, the impact of the contribution increase on the employment and other measures of the economic performance of the economy depends on the extent to which current contributors are confident (or skeptical) that they will receive the promised CPP benefits. If contributors are skeptical that they will receive CPP benefits when they retire, the CPP contribution increase will be perceived as a tax increase and will have a greater negative impact on the economy than if contributors are confident.

Robson also discusses the fragility of the 9.9 percent contribution rate. Robson points out that if the long-term actuarial calculations for the CPP were based on 2.0 percent inflation rate, which seems to be the Bank of Canada's target rate, then the steady-state contribution rate would rise above 9.9 percent.

In my view, the federal government and the provinces have over-sold the notion that the CPP financing problem has been "fixed" and that the rate will never go above 9.9 percent. The federal and provincial governments should have been more circumspect about the durability of the recent reforms and acknowledged that, in the future as in the past, major changes in demographic and economic variables could significantly affect the viability of the CPP. We will have to be flexible and willing to adapt our public pension programs in light of the changing economic and demographic forecasts. For Alberta, the important questions are: would an APP be more or less susceptible to economic and demographic fluctuations? And would an APP be more capable of adjusting its basic parameters as economic and demographic events unfold?

THE QUÉBEC PENSION PLAN: INSTITUTIONAL ARRANGEMENTS AND LESSONS FOR ALBERTA

The chapter by François Vaillancourt (along with the chapter by J.C. Herbert Emery and Kenneth J. McKenzie) provides a brief history of the formation of the CPP and the Québec Pension Plan (QPP). It is interesting to note that the federal and provincial governments decided to set up public pension plans in the early 1960s because of problems with portability of private employment pensions. This reminds us that portability enables workers to change jobs, thereby improving labour market flexibility and enhancing labour productivity. If an APP reduced the portability of pensions, it would be a significant regression.

Vaillancourt highlights 3 aspects of the Québec experience applicable to an APP. I will briefly comment on each of the three aspects, although the conclusions that I draw are not always the ones that Vaillancourt intended.

Lesson 1:
Policy Flexibility Is Enhanced with a Provincial Public Pension Scheme
Vaillancourt points out that Québec was able to tailor the retirement age provisions in the QPP to changes in Québec's retirement age policy. This is an example of the policy flexibility that can be achieved through provincial pension programs. One disappointing aspect of the recent CPP reforms was that the age at which individuals receive full pension benefits was not altered. In view of increasing life-expectancy (see Table 1 on page 71), other countries, ranging from Sweden to the United States, are taking steps to increase the age at which individuals qualify for full public pensions benefits. The failure to address this policy problem in the recent reforms is an example of the adjustment problems that seem to be inherent in a pension scheme where agreement must be reached by seven provinces and the federal government.

Lesson 2:
A Provincial Pension Plan Reduces the Interaction between Federal and Provincial Income Support Programs
Vaillancourt shows that disability benefits have grown much faster under the CPP than under the QPP. Other provinces have an incentive to shift disability cases from provincially funded social assistance/workers' compensation programs to the CPP (where provincial residents bear only a fraction of the total cost of an increase in expenditure)[1]. This off-loading of disability benefits is an example of the perverse incentives created by overlapping federal and provincial programs[2]. However, while a provincial pension plan would discourage provinces from shifting disability expendi-

tures to a national program, such a plan would increase the incentive to shift the costs of pensions to the federal government because cuts to provincial pensions would be off-set by increased expenditures under the federal government's Guaranteed Income Supplement and Spouse's Allowance programs. Pensions will always require interaction between federal and provincial programs, and it is not clear that a provincial pension would reduce the ability of governments to off-load spending.

However, Vaillancourt's discussion of off-loading under overlapping programs raises a different question: why should disability benefits be provided under the CPP? Currently, disability benefits are provided under provincial social assistance and workers' compensation programs, private disability and life insurance coverage, and the CPP. Instead of addressing the off-loading problem by introducing a provincial pension plan, a simpler solution is to remove disability benefits from the CPP.

Lesson 3:
A Provincial Pension Plan Can Be Used for Province-building

Vaillancourt obviously supports the Québec experience of using a public pension investment fund to intervene in capital markets to direct investment and job creation. In my view, the links between the Caisse de dépôts et placements du Québec (CDPQ) and Québec Inc. is the francophone version of the "crony capitalism" practiced in Asia. Québec's rate of economic growth over the past three decades has not been so impressive that these province-building strategies are worth the risks of an Asian-style meltdown. Indeed, Alberta's own experience with province-building or "diversification strategy" in the 1980s resulted in a string of disasters (Novatel, MagCan, and Gainers to name a few). This bitter experience has convinced most Albertans that governments "can't pick winners." In my view, the Québec and Alberta experience with *dirigiste* policies indicates that if Alberta adopts a provincial pension plan, the government must *not* use the investment fund to engage in province-building strategy. The only truly effective way to do that is to avoid the creation of public investment fund, by adopting either PAYGO financing or a system of individually funded and privately managed pensions (along the lines of the Chilean model).

■■■ CHECKING OUT OF THE HOTEL CALIFORNIA: THE DESIRABILITY OF AN ALBERTA PENSION PLAN

Herbert Emery and Kenneth McKenzie analyze two options for an APP—a PAYGO plan that would provide comparable benefits to the existing CPP and a fully funded scheme based on individual retirement accounts. The authors provide a quantitative assessment of the financial implications of these options and discuss the problems that Alberta would encounter in trying to adopt either. These obstacles appear, in their view, to be so overwhelming, that it is unlikely that Albertans would want to "check out" of the CPP.

Emery and McKenzie begin by demolishing an invalid, but frequently cited, reason for an APP—the net outflow of CPP funds from Alberta. Emery and McKenzie argue that the CPP, as with all PAYGO pension schemes, is primarily an *intergenerational redistribution* scheme and not an *interregional redistribution* scheme. Emery and McKenzie then cite three reasons some people give in support of a separate APP:

1. to control Alberta's share of the public pension fund in order to engage in province-building policies;
2. to exploit Alberta's demographic and labour market advantages;
3. to adopt a new type of contributory pension plan.

As I have already indicated in my comments on Vaillancourt's QPP lessons, the first reason gives me heart palpitations. I think that Albertans should be extremely wary of any proposal for an APP that is based on province-building.

At first glance, the second reason, Alberta's relative young population, indicates that a PAYGO APP could provide the equivalent CPP benefits to retired Albertans at contribution rates between 1.0 and 1.75 percent lower than those projected for the CPP. However, the potential for lower contribution rates has to be tempered by a number of considerations.

The first issue is whose pensions the APP will pay. Many former Albertans are now working in or have retired to other parts of Canada, while other retirees now make their home in Alberta. Determining Alberta's share of these pension would undoubtedly require long and protracted negotiations, and the administrative costs of determining the appropriate transfers might be very high. Therefore, the costs of disentangling an APP from the CPP might be prohibitive. Emery and McKenzie conclude the best way for an APP to maintain portability would be to set up private individual retirement accounts (IRAs) so that Albertans could take their pension contributions with them if they left the province. However, Emery and McKenzie did not consider whether other provinces would tax the interest income earned on these Alberta Pension Plan accounts. Such taxes would be a significant deterrent to mobility.

A lower contribution rate may also not materialize because of the additional costs in administering and collecting taxes for an APP. We need to carefully study the administrative costs of an APP to indicate the potential magnitude of any cost increase. I do not think tax collection costs would be a major obstacle. Four other provinces collect employer payroll taxes with relatively low administration and compliance costs, and Alberta has collected provincial health care premiums for many years. Thus the tax collection costs are unlikely to be an insurmountable obstacle, although economies of scale suggest that tax collection costs for an APP would likely be higher than under the CPP, again limiting the potential for lower contribution rates.

Finally, Emery and McKenzie are, in my view, justifiably concerned about the viability of an Alberta Pension Plan in view of the volatility of the Alberta economy. Ted Chambers and Mike Percy have shown that Alberta's economy is the most volatile in North America. The viability of PAYGO pension schemes is affected by the state of the labour market. Financing a large, fixed obligation from the taxes levied on workers in a small, resource dependent economy entails a significant risk. A national pension plan financed by contributions from workers in all regions helps to diversify this economic risk. The higher implicit risk premium implicit in a PAYGO-style APP would further erode the PAYGO contribution rate differential created by Alberta's demographic advantage. We need more information about potential risks caused by our volatile economy and their implications for the contribution rate for an APP before we accept the notion of a "demographic dividend" with an Alberta Pension Plan.

Emery and McKenzie briefly consider the third reason for adopting an APP—the possibility of adopting a fully funded pension scheme based on individual retirement accounts. Regardless of the merits, they detect significant obstacles to this type of scheme because Alberta would have to negotiate with the federal government and the other provinces over how much Alberta would have to contribute toward the unfunded liability of the CPP. The advantages of adopting a compulsory, defined-contribution pension scheme would have to be very clear and compelling before most Albertans would be willing to pursue negotiations over the sharing of the CPP's unfunded liability.

■■■ ALBERTA OPTING OUT OF THE CPP— CAN IT? SHOULD IT?

Robert Brown addresses the two questions posed in his chapter's title. Under the CPP Act, a province is entitled to set up its own provincial pension plan if it is similar to the CPP in terms of benefits and financing. But if an APP has to provide virtually the same benefits at the same contribution rates, then there is no advantage in adopting it. Administration costs may be higher, and there is a potentially larger investment risk if a provincially controlled pension fund is more susceptible than a national pension fund to the political temptation to use the fund for "strategic investments." Brown concludes that any advantage in setting up an APP

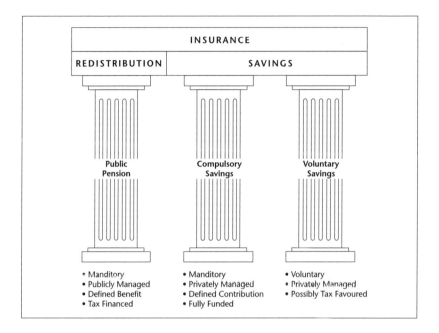

must be because an APP could provide a substantially different pension plan.

The leading candidate for an alternative to the CPP is a system based on compulsory contributions to IRAs. The World Bank (1994) included compulsory contributions to IRAs as one of the "three pillars" of a model public pension system (see Figure 1). The three pillars consist of the following:

1. A mandatory defined benefit public pension scheme. This pillar should be focused on reducing poverty among the elderly. Benefits should be either flat rate (corresponding to a subsistence level of income) or means-tested. Benefits should be financed on a PAYGO basis out of general revenues so that the desired redistribution from rich to poor can be achieved.

2. A mandatory personal savings scheme. This pillar promotes private savings to offset the potential disincentive effect to save because of the first redistributive public pension pillar and the myopic savings decisions of some individuals. The private management of pension funds provides a more efficient allocation of capital in the economy and enhances the prospects for economic growth and employment. As a defined contribution scheme, this pillar would automatically be

fully funded. In retirement, the individual could withdraw the contributions and accumulated investment income at a regulated rate or convert it into an annuity.

3. Voluntary savings. The third pillar of the World Bank's model is voluntary saving by individuals or private occupational pension schemes. The public sector's role is to regulate financial institutions and pension funds and possibly to provide favourable tax treatment for voluntary savings and private occupational pensions.

Together these three pillars perform the redistribution, savings, and insurance functions that are required of a public pension system. Spreading the burden of providing retirement incomes over the three pillars provides individuals with insurance against the longevity, inflation, investment, and political risks that the retired population faces.

The Canadian retirement income system also has three pillars. The Old Age Security program corresponds to the first pillar of the World Bank by providing a basic income safety net. Because it is financed out of general tax revenues, it performs the income redistribution function. The Registered Retirement Savings Plan and the Retirement Pension Plan correspond to the third pillar of the World Bank model by providing tax incentives for voluntary savings for retirement or private employment-related pensions. The Canadian retirement income system deviates from the World Bank's model because the second pillar is the CPP—a compulsory, PAYGO public pension program—not a system of compulsory IRAs.

Brown examines the pros and cons—but mainly the cons—of the IRAs. He bases some comments in part on the Chilean experience with this system. Rather than discussing all of the advantages and disadvantages of a system of IRAs, I will simply comment on a few points Brown raises.

First, Brown contends that fully funded social security systems do not overcome the impact of the impending demographic shocks because the pension income of any decade must come out of the national income of that decade. The method of financing for the public pension system can, however, affect future national income if the financing alters the current level of national savings and therefore the future size of the capital stock in Canada or the amount of Canadians' net claims on foreign assets. Proponents of the IRA approach, such as Martin Feldstein (who has argued for this type of reform in the U.S. in a recent article in *The Economist*), think that switching to an IRA system would significantly increasing savings rates.

Second, Brown highlights the administrative costs—chiefly advertising and commissions—that are 12 to 15 percent of the cashflow into the Chilean funds and therefore much higher than the 1.3 percent expense ratio of the CPP. International comparisons of this type are fraught with problems and are not completely valid because the Chilean system is not as mature as the CPP. Our securities industry is also more mature and may be more efficient and competitive. A more valid comparison is with the expense ratios of the large Canadian mutual funds, which are often as high as 2 percent of assets. If a competitive industry provides a relatively high cost product, this may reflect the value that consumers placed on the service provided by the industry. On the other hand, lack of consumer information may also contribute to excessive sales costs. If an IRA system is adopted, perhaps the appropriate government policy would be to increase consumer information on investment instruments and on the lower cost alternatives to conventional mutual funds.

Third, Brown notes that under an IRA system, Albertans in the transition generation have to pay twice: both to their IRAs and to the unfunded liability of the CPP, which Brown estimates at $50 billion. But under the reformed CPP, the transition generation also pays twice because the 9.9 steady-state contribution rate consists of a (roughly) 7.0 percent component to pay for their own pensions and a 2.9 percent component to pay for the unfunded liability of the CPP. A potential advantage of the IRA system is that it de-links the two components of the transition generation's contributions. The $50 billion dollar unfunded liability could be financed through a variety of means, such as higher personal income taxes, which may be more equitable and more efficient than the payroll tax being used to finance it under the CPP.

Brown also points out that the participation rate in the Chilean compulsory pension plan is relatively low—only 55 percent of the labour force are continuous contributors. The participation rate is low because the guaranteed pension benefits under the first pillar mean that the second pillar, the compulsory contribution to an IRA, does not enhance the pension benefits of a low wage worker to any great degree. Therefore low-wage workers view the compulsory contribution to an IRA as a tax. (Recall Robson's discussion of the importance of whether a pension contribution is perceived to be a tax.) One of the functions of the compulsory contribution to an IRA is to counteract the disincentive to save created by the first pillar. However, the disincentives to work, or at least to work in the above-ground economy, that are created by the interaction of these two pillars has not been fully appreciated. We must pay attention to work incentives as well as savings incentives in designing and assessing the desirability the World Bank's model pension system.

Finally, Brown points out that a compulsory IRA system exposes an individual to investment risk. For example, a major decline in the stock market can greatly reduce the pension benefits from an IRA. This brings out one of the contrasts between a PAYGO system and a compulsory IRA system: as Emery and McKenzie noted, a PAYGO system is vulnerable to labour market shocks while a compulsory IRA system is vulnerable to investment shocks. Since the first pillar of the Canadian pension system, or the World Bank's model system, is financed on a PAYGO basis, there is some diversification of risk if the second pillar is fully funded, especially if the IRAs are invested in an internationally diversified portfolio of assets.

⬛▶ A SUMMING UP

Should Albertans opt out of the CPP? I don't think this is a question we are ready to answer yet. Instead, I offer four points that both summarize the arguments presented in this book and suggest areas of additional research:

1. Replacing the CPP with a PAYGO APP would not substantially reduce contributions.
2. The benefit to moving to an APP may come from increased flexibility and more responsiveness to changes in economic and demographic trends.
3. The most attractive option for an APP would likely be a system of compulsory contributions to IRAs, but disentanglement from the CPP would likely be very costly and create a great deal of uncertainty about individuals' future pensions.
4. We need to analyze the reform of the pension system in the context of our entire network of social programs and economic structures. If nothing else, thinking about an APP forces us think more carefully and more inclusively about pension reform than has been the case in the previous CPP reforms and in the recent ill-fated attempt to reform the Old Age Security system.

Notes
1. This is an example of a vertical fiscal externality, a concept that is receiving increasing attention in the public literature on fiscal federalism. See Dahlby (1996) and Keen (1997).
2. Another area of interdependence is income support programs. It has been claimed that a one-dollar cut to federal employment insurance benefits increases provincial expenditures on social assistance by thirty cents.

References
Dahlby, B. 1996. "Fiscal Externalities and the Design of Intergovernmental Grants." *International Tax and Public Finance* 3, July: 397–412.
Keen, M. 1997. "Vertical Tax Externalities in the Theory of Fiscal Federalism." WP/97/173. Washington, D.C.: Fiscal Affairs Department, International Monetary Fund.
The Economist. 1999. "Martin Feldstein on Social Security." 13 March: 41–43.
World Bank. 1994. *Averting the Old Age Crisis: Policies to Protect the Old and Promote Growth*. A World Bank Policy Research Project. New York: Oxford University Press.